Ancient Irish Legends

Ancient Irish Legends

PADRAIC O'FARRELL

Gill & Macmillan

Gill & Macmillan Ltd
Goldenbridge
Dublin 8
with associated companies throughout the world
© Padraic O'Farrell 1995
0 7171 2252 2
Illustrations by Fiona Fewer
Print origination by Identikit Design Consultants, Dublin
Printed by ColourBooks Ltd, Dublin

A catalogue record is available for this book
from the British Library.

1 3 5 4 2

Contents

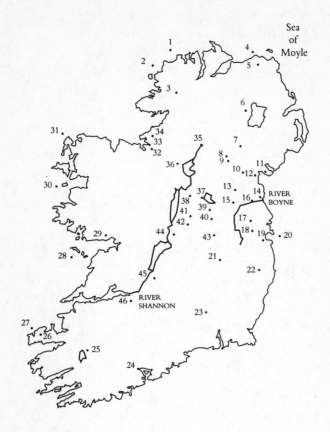

Key to Map of Ireland

To Terry

Introduction

Great tales from Irish mythology can be enjoyed without any background information on their origins. Indeed, some readers may choose to skip this introduction and begin reading the first story. For those who prefer a little preliminary knowledge, the following note is offered.

Old Irish was a Celtic language. Only Latin and Greek predated its literature. Its corpus reflected a mythology written probably as early as the mid-seventh century, but it existed in oral form long before that. Later scholars categorised its sagas and romances as follows:

1. The Mythological Cycle

2. The Red Branch (or Ulster) Cycle

3. The Cycle of Kings

4. The Fenian Cycle

The Mythological Cycle contains sagas of early invaders up to the Milesians and of pre-Christian gods. The Tuatha Dé Danaan (tribes of the Celtic goddess Dana), said to have inhabited Ireland before the arrival of the Celts, feature here. Christian monks chronicled the tales, and therefore acts of godly powers became wondrous escapades of charismatic heroes and heroines. Such euhemerism is common in all cycles.

The celebrated Red Branch Knights, of whom Cuchullain was the most famous, were guardians of Ulster. They billeted at Eamhain Macha, seat of the Ulster king Conor (Conchobhar) Mac Nessa, near Armagh. Mythology depicts them as upright, brave and heroic

warriors. *An Táin Bó Cuailgne* tells of the cattle raid for the
Brown Bull of Ulster (Donn Cuailng) by the Connaght
king and queen, Ailill and Maeve. It is the centrepiece of
the cycle and is Irish mythology's nearest approach to an
epic work like the *Iliad*.

The Cycle of Kings, in particular, mixes myth with
fact. It contains tales of Irish rulers from 300 B.C. to
700 A.D.

The Fenian Cycle is quite straightforward. Fionn Mac
Cumhaill, by receiving his father's magic spear, became
leader of the Fianna, who acted as bodyguards to the High
Kings resident at Tara (Teamhair) in County Meath.
Schoolboys in Irish playgrounds once knew all the qualifications necessary for joining this august body and strove
with little success to match the bodyguards. The trials
included taking a thorn out of a bare foot while running,
bending under a stick held at knee-height without
slowing, and jumping one's own height. Members were
called Fenians and, in either English or Irish, that title has
been adopted by assorted political movements in Irish
history. These include a republican organisation, the
Fenian Brotherhood, founded in New York by John
O'Mahony in 1858; a republican youth movement
(Na Fianna Éireann), founded in Dublin in 1902 by

Countess Markievicz; a political party (Fianna Fáil, founded by Eamon de Valera and others in 1926); and Fianna Uladh (Soldiers of Ulster), a political wing of a splinter group from the IRA, founded in 1953. Some Unionists in Northern Ireland call their Nationalist opponents 'Fenians'. The term Ossianic (after Fionn's son) is often given to the cycle.

Like its Greek counterpart, Irish mythology uses music and literature as means of communication. It inspired the harper and composer Turlough Carolan and composers in Britain, Australia, Germany and the USA. While both traditional and more modern folk songs are often sad laments, the prose in mythological tales is usually spirited, lively and full of proud and noble deeds. It tells the main stories (*príomh-scéil*), concerned with great adventures, military actions, voyages, romances, banquets and tragedies. Lesser stories (*fo-scéil*) relate dreams, chases, deportation, and geological and physical phenomena. Ireland's ancient legislation, the Brehon Laws, laid down strict rules and qualifications for bards. Only the top graduates from bardic colleges who had studied for up to twelve years received permission to recite. When, in the 17th century, the English suppressed these institutions, the Irish *seanchaí* (storyteller) emerged. The tradition survived, but sadly, in this television age, the art is often abused and presented as bucolic buffoonery.

Sources of Irish myth are plentiful. The oldest surviving volume is the *Book of the Dun Cow* (Leabhar na hUidhre), an 11th/12th-century volume written at Clonmacnois, County Offaly. Monks chose this title, tradition says, when they wrote it on vellum from the hide of Saint Ciaran's dark cow. Because it uses 6th- and 8th-century Irish, it is most likely a transcript of earlier

documents. Like the 14th-century *Book of Lecan*, it
contains versions of *An Táin Bó Cuailgne*. Bishop Fionn
McGorman compiled *The Book of Leinster* (Leabhar
Laighneach, also called Leabhar na Nuachonghbála); some
call it *The Book of Glendalough*, after the County Wicklow
monastery where the prelate wrote it in the 12th century.
Another source, Rawlinson Manuscript B502, takes its
name from a Bodleian Library reference. Some scholars
claim that it too originated from Clonmacnois.

Apart from early sources, *Béaloideas*, the journal of the
Folklore Society of Ireland, and manuscript sources of the
Department of Folklore at University College, Dublin
record many tales handed down orally. Writers like
William Carleton, Padraic Colum, Aubrey de Vere, Lady
Gregory, Douglas Hyde, P.W. Joyce, Patrick Kennedy,
Kuno Meyer, Eugene O'Curry, John O'Donovan,
Standish O'Grady, T.F. O'Rahilly, T.W. Rolleston,
J.M. Synge, Lady Wilde and W.B. Yeats have presented
ancient myth and fable in prose, poetic and dramatic
forms. Even today, the characters in Brian Friel's play
Wonderful Tennessee reflect upon another Hy-Brasil or
Tír na nÓg — a strange, mystical somewhere inspired by
ancient myth and fantasy.

There has always been prevarication among scholars
when Ireland's mythology comes under discussion. A
consensus favours the theory that historical fact forms its
basis. This is particularly true in the case of certain characters whose escapades have been romanticised. Whatever
the scholarly interpretation, great tales from Irish
mythology continue to intrigue and entertain.

My selection is a personal one. It does not include
a set number of stories from a given cycle. I retell the
legends in my own words, hoping to entertain rather
than educate.

ONE

The Children of Lir

L ough Derravaragh (Lake of Oaks) in County
Westmeath is set among woodlands and pastures. One
of its inlets, at Knockeyan (Cnocéin — Hill of Birds)
near the town of Mullingar, is steep-sided and tree-
backed, reminding visitors of a miniature Norwegian
fiord. This spot is associated with a popular Irish legend.
Even today, parents name their babies after characters
from the story of the Children of Lir. Tapestries or paintings depicting the fable make popular furnishings.

The fate of the Children of Lir is the second of the
Three Sorrows of Storytelling from Irish mythology.
The other two, concerning the quest of the Sons of
Tuireann and the exile of the Sons of Uisneach, appear
later in this book.

The Tuatha Dé Danaan (tribes of the goddess Dana)
were the gods of pre-Christian Ireland. They inhabited
the land before its final prehistoric invasion by the descen-
dants of the great warrior Milesius. The Milesians defeated
the Tuatha Dé Danaan at the battle of Tailteann. This
spot, at Teltown near Donaghpatrick, County Meath, was
also famous for great harvest festival of Lughnasa, called
after the god Lugh, and for athletic competitions. After
the combat, the vanquished race decided to regroup under
one king. They elected Bódearg of Connaght. This
angered the sea-god Lir, who lived in a fortress called Sí
Fionna, near Newtownhamilton, County Monaghan. Lir
refused to pay homage to the new ruler, so Bódearg's
many supporters vowed to kill the dissenter. Their new
king forbade this, but they ostracised Lir and forced him

to live in seclusion. His misery increased when his wife
Aobh, a beautiful young woman, suddenly died.

Bódearg felt sorry for him and sent a message from
Killaloe, his County Clare seat, offering the choice of his
foster-children as a replacement wife. These were the
daughters of Ailill, the king of the Aran Islands, who were
watched over by that king's loyal charioteer. Highly
pleased by Bódearg's gesture, Lir immediately set out for
Killaloe. A reconciliation with his former colleagues and
a promise of fealty prompted lavish celebrations.
Bódearg invited Lir to inspect the girls — Niamh, Aoife,
and Albha.

Many compared their beauty to three of the four
seasons. Niamh's black hair, white skin and sparkling eyes
reminded Lir of a forest set against the snow and frost of
winter. Aoife had hazel eyes, russet hair, cream skin and the
ripeness of autumn. Albha was as fresh and fair as spring.

After much thought, Lir chose the eldest girl, Niamh.
The marriage ceremony took place in Killaloe and, after
two days of celebration, the couple returned to Sí Fionna
where a great reception awaited them. They settled down
to a blissful married life. Niamh gave birth to twins, a boy
and a girl, Aodh and Fionnuala. The following year
Niamh died while giving birth to twin boys, Conn and
Fiachra. The household at Sí Fionna was devastated; likewise that at Killaloe. Magnanimous again, Bódearg offered
Lir another foster-child, Aoife, as a wife.

Aoife and Lir married and lived happily for a while.
The four children got on well with Aoife and with their
grandfather in Killaloe. They also became very attached to
the King of Aran's charioteer, who had come to Sí Fionna
with Aoife. Bódearg visited often and brought Aodh,
Fionnuala, Conn and Fiachra on holidays to his castle.

Indeed, all the Tuatha Dé Danaan loved them. Their father was very proud of this popularity and doted upon them all the more.

As time passed, however, Aoife became less happy with her situation. She became jealous of her husband's attention to her stepchildren. One day Lir brought Fionnuala a beautiful, gem-encrusted toy chariot for which he had searched the country. Aoife was furious. She still tried to hide her feelings, but every time Lir expressed his love for his children, she became increasingly bitter. This continued until a great hate possessed her. It became so debilitating that she was forced to retire to her bed. The condition of her mind and body deteriorated, and Lir, fearing losing another wife, began to lavish attention on her. Aoife mistook this for pity and screamed angrily at him. Thereafter, during a full year in her darkened room, Aoife plotted a terrible deed that she thought would regain all Lir's love for herself.

She surprised him one day by jumping out of bed and resuming her household duties. She appeared to be back to normal. Lir's heart felt light and he went away on a hunting trip. While he was gone, Aoife announced that she intended to visit Killaloe with the children. Three of them cheered with delight, but Fionnuala was apprehensive. The night before, she had dreamed that her stepmother had placed a curse upon them. Fionnuala's anxiety grew when her grandfather's loyal charioteer whispered a warning to her to stay behind. He had noticed Aoife's jealousy and demeanour closely enough to suspect her of some evil intent.

Unfortunately, Aoife arrived before Fionnuala could run away, so they all set out on the journey. After crossing Monaghan and Cavan, they entered Westmeath. As the

retinue rested, Aoife took the charioteer aside and
promised him wealth and security if he would kill the
children and dispose of their bodies. He refused, as did
other retainers whom the wicked stepmother approached.
Furiously, she ordered the party to continue. As they
passed between the village of Crookedwood and the town
of Mullingar, she called upon her servants to camp for the
night. They halted on the shore of Lough Derravaragh.
Aoife planned to kill the children herself, but when she
raised her spear to strike at Conn, she could not bring
herself to deliver the death-thrust.

There was still plenty of daylight, so she encouraged
the children to undress and go for a swim. As each small,
naked body passed by her, she touched it with a druidic
rod saying, 'Live then! Not as a child, but as a swan!'

Four beautiful swans swam from the shore as Aoife
spoke an incantation:

This curse I place upon you:
Linger three hundred years upon this lake;
Three hundred on the Sea of Moyle,
Three hundred on the Western Ocean by Erris,
Until the woman from the south will wed the man from the north
And a cold bell peals,
Bringing belief in the word of God throughout the land.

The deed was done and almost immediately the stepmother was sorry. Her curse could not be undone, but in
pity for their loneliness, she cast a second spell which
granted the swans human intelligence and the use of
speech and song.

Foolishly, Aoife carried on to Killaloe, where her
foster-father questioned her about the children. She lied,
saying that Lir again was refusing fealty to Bódearg.

Bódearg did not believe her and sent a messenger to Lir. The sea-god became distraught when he heard that his children were missing. Remembering Aoife's year in bed, he feared for her sanity and wondered if she might have killed them. Quickly, he ordered the harnessing of chariots and set out for Killaloe.

Lir too camped by Derravaragh. When the sun was setting, casting a shimmering pinkness across the lake's waters, he heard the most beautiful singing coming from behind an expanse of high reeds. Four elegant swans swam into view and one spoke to him, saying that she was his daughter, Fionnuala. She explained what had happened. People told of trees across the land bending from the force of Lir's lamentation.

In the meantime, the charioteer informed Bódearg of Aoife's wickedness. He too had a druidic rod, with which he struck his foster-daughter, turning her into a demonic hag, a Morrígan. She soared up into the sky, and was never seen again.

When Lir arrived in Killaloe, the two men shared their sorrow for three days. Bódearg issued a decree that a swan was never to be killed in Ireland (and to this day, superstition deems it unlucky to do so). The Munster king called a mighty conclave of the Tuatha Dé Danaan on the shores of Derravaragh. Word spread and the Milesians came too. The throng covered the slopes of nearby Cnocéin and spent many nights listening to the sweetest singing they had ever heard. By day, they conversed with the Children of Lir.

Life for the swan children continued like this for three hundred years, when the curse demanded that they should fly to the Sea of Moyle between Ireland and Scotland. They departed with trepidation and sadness for, in spite of their feathered form, they had enjoyed their time on the lake.

On the Sea of Moyle, they were cold and hungry. Great waves tossed them about; the north winds blew cold. One bad day, black clouds indicated that a great storm was bearing down. The four named a meeting-place in case the swell should separate them. They did indeed fail to remain together, and after a night of being hurled through the air and lashed by waves, Fionnuala headed for the agreed spot, Carrignarón, Rock of the Seals. She awaited the others and when they did not appear she sang a lament, thinking they had perished. Yet one by one they arrived, bedraggled and weary.

Their misery on the Sea of Moyle continued, although sometimes they ventured into the river estuaries of Ireland and Scotland. Once, on the river Bann, near where Belfast now stands, horsemen of the Tuatha Dé Danaan spotted them. Bódearg had ordered them to search for the four. Long time-lapses and abnormal life spans are common in mythology, but nonetheless this meeting was an exciting event. The soldiers told the swans that all their relatives and friends in Killaloe, Sí Fionna and around Lough Derravaragh were well. The four swans sent their greetings in song and returned to complete their three-hundred-year sentence on the inhospitable wild sea.

When they departed, their route to the Western Ocean took them across places in Ireland that they had loved. They flew as high as they could to avoid seeing them. Still, they could not escape the sadness of noticing their childhood home at Sí Fionna, greatly deteriorated, and the pleasant waters of Lough Derravaragh. With heavy hearts they landed near Erris Head in County Mayo.

Warmed by the gentle Gulf Stream, their new place of penance was less severe, but although the storms that raged across the Atlantic Ocean were fewer, they were more intense than those on the Sea of Moyle. Towards the end of their three hundred years, a young man heard the songs of the Children of Lir, became enchanted by them and spent weeks listening to the story of their plight. Irish lore credits this farmer, Abhric, with handing down the popular fable, for he alone heard it in its entirety. If so, he recorded only one matter of significance from their second exile — that during it the children learned about God, and about the Christian faith. They enjoyed this privilege in the years before Saint Patrick came to Ireland's shores.

When at last they had completed their sentence, the four swans flew back to Sí Fionna. Their father's mansion was a ruin. They wept and composed another lament before returning to seek Abhric's advice. As soon as they asked for it, they heard a church bell ringing, and remembered that their wicked stepmother had given this as a sign that her evil curse would be lifted. The swans immediately began to sing more beautifully than ever. They did not realise that it was the year 432. Saint Patrick had arrived in Ireland and had sent the bell-ringer to find the Children of Lir. This man, Mocaemhoch, followed the sound of their song, befriended them and brought them to his hermitage. He bound them with specially crafted silver chains so that when they swam off Erris, they would remain together. He told them about Christianity and they became very happy in his company. His greatest problem was controlling the crowds that travelled from afar to hear their incredibly sweet singing.

Word of this wonder spread to Fionnín, King of Munster, whose daughter, Deocha, was to marry Connaght's King Lairgneán. Fionnín had always spoiled his daughter and, when she expressed a wish to own the

singing swans, he demanded them from the King of
Connaght, in whose seas they swam. Lairgneán sent his
soldiers to fetch them. First they tried to buy them from
Mocaemhoch. The hermit refused but, even with Abhric's
assistance, he failed to prevent the Connaght soldiers from
seizing the bound swans and taking them away to
Munster. The loyal couple followed, hoping to find some
way of recovering them.

Deocha and her father had come to collect their prize
at Killaloe where the Children of Lir had once spent such
happy times. Their laying eyes upon the swans represented
the exact moment for Aoife's curse to expire. The bell had
already pealed and now the woman from the South was to
marry the man from Connaght which, although in the
west of Ireland, was north of Munster. As captors and
faithful former guardians looked on, the soft white feathers
fell away and the Children of Lir re-emerged, not as
bright, lively youths, but as nine-hundred-year-old
wretches. Horrible to behold, they lived for only a few
moments, during which, in a croaky voice, Fionnuala
begged Mocaemhoch to give the four the sacrament of
baptism. She requested burial in the same protective
formation they had kept when swimming on the dread
Sea of Moyle. This was granted. They laid Fionnula in a
communal grave with Conn on her right, Fiachra on her
left, and Aodh at her head.

Some versions of the story end without further
elaboration. Others claim that, just as the ravaged creatures
died, Mocaemhoch saw a vision in the sky — of a pretty
laughing girl and three handsome young boys. At that
moment he realised why he had been told to find the four
singing swans. Saint Patrick wanted him to be at hand to
save their souls when the evil spell was lifted.

TWO

Conán's Woolly Body

The Fianna were a band of warriors who acted as bodyguards to the High Kings of Ireland. Their headquarters was a fortress on the Hill of Allen, the only tor of significance among the plains of County Kildare. Conán (Wolf) Mac Mórna was an unpopular member of the Fianna, ugly, obese, and given to backbiting and jeering. Since he was bald, his colleagues often called him Conán Maol. Consistently he broke the tradition of generosity that prevailed among the Fianna, particularly concerning food. A glutton, he was always the last to leave the big table in the refectory. Unlike the others, he never removed his clothing, and everyone knew why; his body was covered with coarse, black wool instead of hair. This is how it happened.

Hunting in a strange forest one day, the Fianna happened upon a wide, bright track that led them to an impressive green-roofed palace whose walls were of some strange texture that sparkled. Curiosity drove them to call a greeting through its open door, but they received no reply. They entered, and in the main dining room saw a huge table laden with *sean gach dí agus núa gach bia* (the oldest of drink and the freshest of food). There was silver tableware and the dishes were piled high as if for a banquet. The Fianna sat down and began to eat and drink their fill.

One of them noticed the expensively draped wall opposite him turn to coarse tree bark. Another screamed as he spotted the ceiling moving slowly downwards. A third saw the other three walls closing in and shouted to his fellow warriors to evacuate the enchanted building quickly.

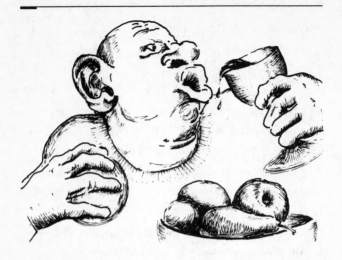

They spilled food and wine as they dashed for the
door, jumping across the table and knocking over benches
in their haste. The second last man out looked back from
the doorway and spotted Conán the Bald still stuffing
himself with food, even though he knew he was unsafe.
Calling two friends, this man went back and tried to pull
the intemperate oaf from his stool. He was stuck!

The walls kept closing in and the ceiling now was
almost touching their heads. They gave a last mighty
heave and released Conán, but left his clothes and some
of his skin stuck to the stool. They laid him in the forest
outside, his raw flesh glistening in the sun, just like the
palace walls. A shepherd, wending his way homeward,
kindly offered a fleece from a black sheep to cover the
unfortunate Conán. It grafted itself on, and that is how the
glutton of the Fianna became woolly.

THREE

Cuchullain and Ferdia

The Irish name for Ardee in County Louth is *Áth Ferdia*, Ferdia's Ford. Here two great heroes met in single combat and established a legend that was as heartbreaking as it was noble. Brother fighting brother, friend against friend — the accounts of Ireland's wars contain many instances of honourable obligations displacing affinity. The story of Cuchullain (the Hound of Ulster) and Ferdia (Godman), his foster-brother, epitomises these.

Ferdia was the son of Daman, one of the Firbolgs whose pre-Christian invasion of Ireland preceded that of the Milesians. As youths, both he and Cuchullain had attended the military school run by Scáthac, a formidable Scottish female warrior, on the Isle of Skyne, thought to be the present-day Isle of Skye. Cuchullain, originally called Setanta, was a skilled hurler and, although he had many competitive games with Ferdia, the pair never fell out. During their training, they got into many fights, but they always stood by each other and were never beaten.

The years passed and they grew to manhood. When the time came for them to return to Connaght and Ulster, their respective provinces in Ireland, they were sad at parting. They embraced and promised to remain firm friends.

Ailill and Maeve, king and queen of Connaght, boasted about their respective properties. In castles, jewels, land and livestock they were equal, but Ailill's white bull surpassed everything. This animal, Finnbheanach (White-horned), had been bred from a heifer in Maeve's herd.

A reincarnated swineherd, Finnbheanach abandoned his
flock because he refused to be owned by a woman. Maeve
was intent on acquiring a superior beast, but the only
possible contender was the Brown Bull of Ulster. She sent
her steward to hire or buy it and authorised him to pay
well. Some say she even offered to sleep with Daire
MacFachtna, the Ulster owner of the bull. Daire was
delighted and agreed to hire the bull for fifty heifers, some
land and a chariot. At the mention of a possible liaison
with Maeve, he winked at the steward.

When the deal had been made, the pair had a few
drinks with Daire's farmhands. All agreed that Daire was a
decent man. Then the Connaght emissary foolishly
boasted that if Daire had not consented, Maeve would
have brought an army to take the bull by force. As they
say in Ireland, that put the *caibosh* (way of death) on it.
Daire's chief herd overheard the remark and told his
master, who promptly cancelled the deal.

The steward returned to Maeve and admitted that he
had blundered. He was afraid of being punished, but
Maeve commended him and said she would prove him
right. She assembled a vast army and marched on Ulster to
seize the Brown Bull. That great epic of Irish mythology
An Táin Bó Cuailgne (The Cattle Raid of Cooley)
describes the progress of the event. The belligerents joined
in single combat and in massed battles. They made and
broke pacts, spied on each other and attempted
infiltrations and seductions.

Cuchullain was prominent in all the more noble
operations. One by one he slaughtered the great warriors
of Connaght, once beheading a dozen of them together.
Few were aware that he was using the *gae bolga* (belly
spear), given to him by his Scottish mentor, Scáthac. He

hurled this dreadful weapon at each opponent with his foot. When it entered the body, it opened into barbs and mutilated the innards. Maeve became frustrated.

Meanwhile Ferdia was lurking in his tent, far away from the action and from Maeve and Ailill. He did not wish to engage in combat with his boyhood friend. At dawn each day he sent an observer to the battleground. After sunset, he listened with admiration to accounts of Cuchullain's prowess. Often he contemplated the possibility of rushing to his assistance, should that be required. Ferdia's reticence did not go unnoticed, and soon Maeve's soldiers began to complain, 'Our colleagues are being annihilated, yet Ferdia, our best fighter, is malingering.' They told Maeve that Ferdia's horny skin would protect him from the *gae bolga* and that in every other way he was Cuchullain's equal. She listened carefully and then sent for Ferdia. He refused her summons, so she ordered her best bards to Ferdia's tent to sing insulting songs, accusing him of disloyalty and cowardice. After several days and nights of this scorn, Ferdia agreed to meet Maeve and her husband.

They named an evening and prepared a great feast, seating Ferdia at the top table, between Queen Maeve and her daughter Finnabhair. By arrangement, Finnabhair plied Ferdia with wine and kisses and seduced him by opening the top of her dress. At the same time, Maeve kept telling him of his bravery and skill at arms, saying that the whole world knew about his valour. She promised him land and possessions — golden rings and brooches, chariots and exemptions from levies for himself and his kinsfolk. As Finnabhair looked into Ferdia's eyes and promised him undying love, Maeve whispered in his ear. She guaranteed her daughter's hand in marriage if Ferdia would fight Cuchullain.

The flattery and drink almost worked. Ferdia leered lasciviously at his temptress and was about to accept her mother's bribes when he changed his mind. The diners seethed when they heard him recite a poem in praise of Cuchullain and of their undying friendship.

Disappointed but undaunted, Maeve feigned a casual conversation with the dinner guests opposite. Lying, she said that Cuchullain was telling everybody that Ferdia had more sense than to try to fight him. Where promises of wealth and love had failed, hurt pride succeeded. With a mighty roar, Ferdia vowed to face Cuchullain the following morning.

After drinking more wine, Ferdia retired and slept well. Cuchullain did not, because a former Ulsterman in Maeve's army, Fergus, crept across the lines to tell him that Ferdia had agreed to fight him to please a woman. All night the Hound of Ulster agonised. In the morning, he even stayed in bed late in case he would reveal his anxiety to his fellow soldiers.

Ferdia was waiting at the ford on the Boyne near Ardee when Cuchullain arrived in his chariot. Ferdia welcomed his old friend, but Cuchullain snubbed him, saying, 'There are two reasons why you should not bid me welcome, Ferdia. First, it is bad manners to wait for me on *my* territory. Secondly, you have placed the love of a woman before our sworn friendship.'

Yet despite these aggressive words, Cuchullain's heart was not in the fight and he cast aside his trusty *gae bolga*. Ferdia too was unenthusiastic. They parried and thrust all day, but neither man drew blood because their efforts were so half-hearted. Whenever their eyes met, each noticed pain in the other's. Evening came and they stopped for the night. Throwing their weapons aside, they

embraced. Their charioteers had made beds of rushes for
them. Cuchullain's brought him herbal oils and magic
potions to ease his aching limbs and he told him to bring
the same to Ferdia. Ferdia's prepared the choicest food
and the two friends shared it.

There was plenty of bloodshed on the second day,
because they abandoned their small spears for
broadswords. The clash of steel sounded all over Ireland
and that evening their bodies were covered with gaping
wounds. With tears in their eyes, they tended these.
Cuchullain soaked moss in boar's dung and applied the
healing poultice to Ferdia's injuries. He responded by
covering Cuchullain's wounds with spiders' webs. These
old treatments worked and they were ready to continue
the fight at dawn. Or so it seemed! Ferdia had lost more

blood than his opponent and the midday sun tired him
quickly. His friend noticed, but had not the heart to
follow up his advantage. They contented themselves with
feigning a fight for the remainder of that day.

While they rested, Cuchullain reminded Ferdia of
their youth and begged him to give up. Ferdia refused. He
had given his word to his people and could not renege.
That night they parted and slept in separate tents.

On the fourth day Ferdia wore a leather and iron suit,
warning Cuchullain that there would be no holds barred.
They fought so fiercely that their shields were battered;
they cast them aside and continued. Birds screamed in the
air and animals scattered under the ferocity.

The pair struggled so much in the Boyne that its
course was changed and its waters ran red with blood.
Hacked pieces of flesh lay on fields and hedgerows.
Towards evening, Ferdia saw an opening and plunged his
sword three times into his friend's body. He took a few
paces back to deliver his *coup de grâce*. As he did, one of
Cuchullain's seconds handed the Ulsterman the *gae bolga*
and he cast it with all the force he could muster. It tore
through Ferdia's mail and dug itself deep into his chest.
The fight was over.

Cuchullain uttered a great wail, then rushed and gath-
ered his friend into his arms. He bore him to the Ulster
side of the river. Despite warnings that Maeve's army
would come and destroy him, Cuchullain stayed by
Ferdia's dead body all night. His laments echoed as far
away as Scotland, where his ageing mentor, Scáthac, heard
them and she too was overcome with grief.

FOUR

Díarmuid and Gráinne

A ll over Ireland, certain cromlechs, mounds or single large stones are called *Leaba Dhíarmada agus Gráinne* (Díarmuid and Gráinne's bed) or *Leaba na Caillighe* (the Bed of the Hag). The couple mentioned are probably the most glamorous lovers in ancient Irish legend. He was strikingly handsome, she was the most elegant and beautiful woman in the land.

The god of love, Aengus Óg, fostered Díarmuid. Unaware of the dire fate that awaited him, the youth matured and became a prominent member of the Fianna warrior band. His father, Roc, discovered his wife having an affair with Aengus Óg's steward. She gave birth to a son, but Roc killed the infant and used his druid's staff to turn the tiny corpse into a savage boar. For further revenge, he ordered the boar to kill Díarmuid if it ever came across him.

When he grew up, Díarmuid adopted some of his mother's traits. Once he was hunting with three of the Fianna when they asked shelter of an old man. He regaled them with wise parables. When the four young men retired, the man's beautiful young daughter stole into their room. All four tried to make love to her, but she chose Díarmuid. He must have given her pleasure because she placed a *ball seirce* or beauty spot on his forehead. She told him that she was the Goddess of Youth and that the spot would ensure that no woman could ever resist making love to him.

Gráinne was the daughter of the celebrated High King of Ireland, Cormac Mac Art, who may have ruled the

country as late as the third century. She received many
offers of marriage, but refused them all. Her household
wanted her to wed the ageing and widowed Fionn Mac
Cumhaill. The spirited young woman did not relish the
idea, but an ambiguous answer to Oisín, who conveyed
Fionn's proposal, led to wedding arrangements being
made. Only during a banquet that preceded the nuptials
did she become fully aware of Fionn's plans. She cast her
eye around the table for a likely replacement groom. As
soon as she noticed the beauty spot on Díarmuid, she was
smitten and determined to elope with him.

When Fionn and his warriors had drunk to excess,
Gráinne called her own servant girl and told her to fill the
largest *meidir* (drinking cup) with wine and bring it to her.
The girl obeyed and Gráinne cast a spell on it. There were
four handles on these square vessels and Gráinne offered
one to Fionn. He drank and, as was customary, presented
it to the queen, who in turn passed it on to the next
highest in rank. One by one, the drinkers fell asleep. This
went on until the cup came to Díarmuid. Before he could
raise it to his lips, Gráinne had them otherwise attracted.
She kissed him and begged him to take her away and
make love to her.

Díarmuid was in a tight spot. He wished to remain
loyal to Fionn, but the rules of the Fianna stated that a
woman's love should not be refused. His friends, Oisín,
Oscar and Fionn's cousin Caoilte Mac Rónan, had not
drunk from the cup, so he asked their advice. They told
him to go with Gráinne, because they were romantics at
heart and knew that Fionn was too old for the girl.
Díarmuid was not convinced. He offered Gráinne a weak
excuse, saying that since Fionn was asleep, all the gates
around the fortress would be locked and guarded.

'Not the secret wicket gate in my garden,' Gráinne said with a wink that made Díarmuid think she was speaking euphemistically. His manhood aroused, he responded. Gráinne led her lover away into the night. There was great commotion when the spell wore off and Fionn and his party awoke to find the pair missing. The great leader was furious and ordered the Fianna to track them down and kill his disloyal henchman. They would have no part in what they regarded as an old man's act of jealousy, so Fionn hired assorted mercenaries.

The lovers roamed all over Ireland, always fearing capture. Some accounts say they made passionate love in the 'beds' called after them. Others hold that, for a long time, Díarmuid's guilt prevented him from succumbing to Gráinne's seduction. They claim that Díarmuid even left subtle signs that would convince the pursuing Fionn that this was so.

Whenever the band of mercenaries attempted to capture or kill him, Díarmuid fought them off easily. Sometimes he humiliated his attackers. Once he left them trussed in pairs like fowl ready for slaughter. Over meadow and moor the fugitives wandered; where they cooked they did not eat, where they ate they did not sleep. Eventually Díarmuid grew tired of being pursued. He built a hut of sally rods and rushes and planted a defensive paling cut from high poplar trees. There, some say, the couple made such wild love that the birds of the forest trilled in elaborate harmony and warm winds whispered wondrous words of passion across the mountainside.

A tribe called Nevin came across this structure. One climbed a tree and saw Gráinne brushing her hair and Díarmuid sharpening a spear. He told the others and they reported the sighting to Fionn. He and a few of the

Fianna came back with the Nevins and surrounded the
enclosure. Fionn ordered two men to position themselves
at each of its six gates. He himself stood at the seventh.
Foolishly, he allotted guard duties to the Fianna.

Aengus Óg saw the lovers' plight and came to spirit
them away. Díarmuid would not leave, but he allowed his
foster-father to take Gráinne to a safe place called *Ros Dhá
Roshoileach* (Two Swallows Headland, thought to have been
in County Limerick). He prepared to fight his way out.

Approaching one gate Díarmuid called, 'Who is on
guard out there?'

It was Oscar and Oisín. They offered to let him
escape if he opened the gate, but he would not accept the
easy option. The same thing happened at the second exit,
where Caoilte stood guard. At every gate, indeed,
Díarmuid was offered an escape route. He refused,
fearing that Fionn would exact revenge on his friends
for helping him. So, at the seventh gate, he faced
Fionn himself. Or so it seemed when they called out
to each other!

Díarmuid had kept a spare pole when he built the
paling and he vaulted over the waiting Fionn, his cohorts
and the Nevins. It happened so quickly that they did not
even see him and while they were still waiting for him to
come out, he was enjoying suckling pig with his foster-
father and Gráinne at Two Swallows Headland.

After this adventure, Díarmuid realised that there was
only one place where he might find peace: Blackwood in
County Mayo. The thick green forest contained a quicken
tree that bore magic berries. It had grown there after a
fairy hurling team had played against the Fianna many
years before and a supporter had dropped a berry by
mistake. This grew into a tree that was guarded by a fierce

giant called *Searbhán Lochlannach* (the Bitter Marauder).
Everybody, including Fionn, avoided this place. Díarmuid
asked the giant to allow them to stay in the wood in
return for a promise never to touch the berries. The giant
agreed, because he realised that the mighty Díarmuid
would be a formidable friend.

Fionn heard about this and secured the aid of two
men known as the Sons of Morna who were trying to
enlist in the Fianna. He offered them admission if they
brought him back Díarmuid's head or a fistful of berries.
They set off for Blackwood, where they met Díarmuid
and told him their story. Gráinne overheard it and became
interested in the fruit. The men opted for fighting
Díarmuid instead of the giant, but he had no trouble
beating their heads together and tying them up. He had
considerable trouble, however, trying to talk Gráinne out
of an impulsive longing for the forbidden fruit. She
goaded him and, although he knew the giant could be
overcome by one blow of his own weapon, he gave in.
The Mornas begged for their release so that they could see
the encounter.

Politely, Díarmuid asked the giant for some fruit, but
he roared his refusal and charged at Díarmuid. They wrestled, kicked and tore at each other until *Searbhán
Lochlannach* stumbled. Díarmuid whipped the club from
his hand and struck him on the head three times. The
giant toppled over. When he hit the ground, so great was
the thud, apples from every tree in Ireland fell. Berries
from the tree fell too. Díarmuid picked up some and gave
them to the Mornas.

The rogues ran back to Fionn with the berries, but he
smelt Díarmuid's hand off them and chastised his hirelings
for trying to deceive him. Then he and a few followers
went to Blackwood, but could see nobody near the tree.

Díarmuid and Gráinne had taken over the giant's home in
the branches and were busy eating the magic fruit. To pass
the time, Fionn played chess with Oisín. He had almost
beaten him, but Díarmuid had been watching from above
and he lobbed a berry on the piece that would win the
game for Oisín. This happened three times and then Fionn
roared a challenge into the tree-top. Again, Aengus came
to Gráinne's rescue and spirited her to a safe place. As
before, Díarmuid sprang across the waiting mob and ran to
join his foster-father and Gráinne at Brúgh na Bóinne (the
Boyne Mansion, or Newgrange, County Meath). There
they remained until Aengus went to Fionn and asked him
to make peace. Old and weary from all the chasing, Fionn
agreed. The couple got married and received valuable gifts
and property before settling down at Rathgraney, near
Tara, County Meath. Four sons and a daughter were born
before the couple invited Fionn and Cormac Mac Art to
dinner one day. Gráinne wanted to find out if the feud was
fully forgotten, so she encouraged the men to go hunting.

Fleet-footed as they were, they soon reached Ben
Bulben in Sligo, where Fionn noticed that a vicious boar
was following them. He encouraged Díarmuid to fight it.
Fionn leered when the boar rammed his tusks into
Díarmuid's stomach. The valiant warrior had met his fate
from his stepbrother. There was only one hope. He knew
that water dropped into his mouth from Fionn's hands had
the power to heal his wound. He asked Fionn but,
although there was a well nearby, the old man refused.
Díarmuid died. Colleagues bore his corpse back to Meath
for burial. Aengus Óg attended and gave Gráinne the dead
body that he promised her would speak to her each day.

The Fianna resented it greatly when Gráinne eventually became Fionn's wife. And no wonder!

FIVE

Another Side of Conán

Although Conán Maol was an unpopular glutton, his strength and toughness often saved the day for the Fianna. One autumn evening Fionn and the Fianna were hunting a magic deer that used to appear once every seven years around their fortress. They had often tried to catch it, but had never succeeded. This time, they released all their hounds, but even Bran and Sceolan, Fionn's nephew and niece in animal form, were not fast enough and soon they lost the scent. Fifteen of the warriors went to the west side of the Hill of Allen to play chess and forget their disappointment. Among them were Oisín, Díarmuid, Oscar and Conán Maol, the Fianna's best fighters.

Suddenly a huge giant appeared before them, dressed in animal-skins. He hailed Oisín and invited him, Fionn and his seven battalions to a banquet and assorted entertainments.

'These will last until May Day,' he promised. Conán's eyes lit up, but he knew he would have more to eat if the guest list was restricted, so he said, 'Thanks, giant, but don't bother asking Fionn or the rest of the Fianna. They are on the other side of the hill listening to a bard praising their valour. Their vanity will keep them there for some time. We are the best of the Fianna, and having us to dinner is as good as having the whole band. Furthermore, the fare will be so plentiful for the few that all those bards and balladeers will turn to singing your praises instead.'

The ploy worked. The giant gave each of them an apple and led them away. Conán bit into the fruit and declared that it was far sweeter than the finest music. The giant boasted that he had seven orchards laden with the same apples which Conán and the others could eat to their hearts' content until May Day. He also bragged that he was such a fast runner that they might not be able to keep up with him.

Conán lied, saying 'Did I not keep up with the enchanted deer a short time past?' With that, the giant began running over field and forest, across sea and lakeshore until they arrived at his house.

'Go inside the lot of you and put on a good fire while I get the food,' the giant ordered.

They went in, but began complaining among themselves. Conán, in particular, thought the food should have been cooked before their arrival. He set a fire and lit it, but no smoke came from it. Oisín said, 'I have been inside every house in Ireland in my time but never this one. I don't think we are in Ireland at all.'

The thirteen others agreed with him, but Díarmuid said he thought he remembered something about it. 'Go outside, one of you, and see is there a boulder in the yard near the door. If there isn't, then I am as ignorant about our whereabouts as the rest of you.' Conán went out, discovered the rock and returned with the news. Díarmuid then told a story.

'Once I hunted in this area with Fionn and the Fianna. He and I let the others continue chasing boars and stags and we lay down here for a rest. Fionn fell asleep and must have had a nightmare, for he lashed out with his foot and struck me in the chest. I coughed up blood and, in my anger, threw stones at him. His two feet were bleeding and blood was flowing from his mouth. He jumped up and charged at me, but I stopped him with my shield. Then he cooled down and said, "I know I nearly killed you. I dreamt that the Tuatha Dé Danaan built a great house on this site and that they would capture all the Fianna here one day and harm them grievously." I believe this to be the house that Fionn was speaking about.'

While they were listening to this account, the giant ran back to Fionn and the rest of his warriors and offered them the same invitation. 'Who are you, that is so decent?' he asked the giant.

'A great admirer of yours. My name is Dearg Mac Donnarta.'

'Your offer of hospitality until May Day is a noble one, Dearg, but if we go for that length of time we will have to take our womenfolk, children and livestock — even our druids and bards.'

'All will be welcome. Come as soon as you can,' the giant said before departing.

Fionn and his followers arrived at the house in ones

and twos. It was not the house where the other fifteen were. Fionn washed his hands and spent a while sucking his thumb for inspiration (the next story will divulge how this gave him wisdom). He realised that Conán and the others were in danger. After warning his warriors to follow him later, he left the house. As soon as he had arrived at the house where the fifteen were, the giant returned, leered at Fionn and said, 'You own this house now, but three hundred of my best warriors surround it this minute, so you must offer them hospitality.' Fionn did this and after a few minutes the giant said there were as many more outside seeking admission.

'Let them all in,' Fionn said, even though he sensed a growing danger to himself and his colleagues.

'An ugly hag and three hundred female champions now wish to join us,' the giant said.

These women carried bows and arrows. All over Ireland, people acknowledged their deadly aims. Fionn ordered them to sit together opposite the small band of the Fianna, then appointed Conán doorkeeper for the night.

'I will not let anybody in without your permission,' Conán promised. Very soon, an ugly reprobate approached him. Coarse black hair reached to his waist and prickly eyebrows covered most of his filthy face. His nose was crooked and dirty, his sunken black eyes were beady and black. When he demanded admission, Conán got clearance from Fionn. As soon as he had eaten, the rogue issued a challenge: 'Let the best man here stand before me and I will eject him from this house.'

'Our best fighter let you in a moment ago,' Fionn answered. With that, the oaf rushed at Conán, tackled him below the knees and tossed him through the door. Conán landed in a puddle of dirty water. Furious, he leaped up and charged. The pair wrestled and elbowed, bit and punched each other from one end of the huge refectory to the other.

Conán began to get the upper hand, but his opponent tried to touch him with a charm of poison. Conán spotted the ruse, drew his sword and cut the stranger in two. With that, the old hag jumped to her feet. She attacked Conán and a fierce scuffle ensued. Eventually she tied up Conán, carried him outside and landed him in the dirty water again. Such disgrace for the champion of the Fianna! He was almost crying when he called out to Díarmuid to untie him.

Fionn would not allow this because to accept help in a contest was dishonourable. So Conán contracted his muscles and induced all his strength from his trunk to his shoulders, from his shoulders to his elbows and from his elbows to his hands. Perspiration spilled from his forehead and added so much water to the puddle that he almost drowned. Then he uttered a mighty roar and burst free of his bonds. Rushing back in, he faced the hag once more.

She wiped wine from her lips and goaded him, saying 'Do you know why I did not cut your head off?'

'Because you were afraid.'

'How dare you suggest such a thing! I will tell you the reason. Once upon a time I was Fionn Mac Cumhaill's housekeeper for a year. During that period you were just a silly young lad ogling me and trying to court me. You were a scrawny bit of a weasel with less meat on you than you'd see on a tinker's stick after a row at a fair. I wouldn't be bothered with you. Yet, for old time's sake, I did not finish you off just now.'

Whether Conán remembered or not, is not clear, but he grabbed the wench, threw her to the ground and drew his sword to behead her.

'Stop! I have a present for you,' she screamed.

'What?'

'You see my three hundred followers? The arrows they shoot cannot miss. Each one kills the man who feels the slightest desire for the archer. Now if you preserve me, I will order them to break their alliance with your enemies.'

Conán asked Fionn what he should do.

'Never refuse assistance offered,' Fionn counselled.

Conán accepted the advice and told the hag to get up. She did, then called her followers and they all marched away. They were hardly out of sight when a savage-looking reprobate arrived with a big hound on a chain. When this black monster gnashed its teeth, huge sparks flew and almost singed Conán's whiskers. Its master called out, 'I hear the Fianna never refuse a request for fight. All I ask is a match for my hound.'

Conán laughed so loudly that trees as far away as Scotland swayed as if blown by a great wind.

'How dare you issue such a stupid challenge! The Fianna have the best dogs in Ireland.'

He whistled for his own wolfhound. Normally this huge brute would have no trouble disposing of the other, but there was a spell on the stranger's dog and after a few barks and bites, Conán's hound lay dead at his feet. Conán was heartbroken and angry and vowed that some day he would behead the owner of the dog.

One by one, the dogs of the other fifteen fought the phantom beast. He savaged each in turn until only Fionn's thoroughbred, Bran, remained. Incredibly, for he was a brave dog, Bran whimpered and rubbed against his master's legs in fear. He asked his uncle not to pit him against the big black hound. Fionn encouraged

him, recalling his great feat against an Offaly bear at
Croghan Hill and how he had saved the Fianna from a
magic wildcat of Slieve Gullion. Pride surged through
the dog's veins. His neck-hairs stood on end and he
shook himself, sprang to his feet snarling, and boldly
faced his adversary.

It was a bloody encounter. Good and all as Bran was,
the spell on the dog that faced him was strong and tiring
to contend with. Díarmuid noticed this, so he separated
the dogs and took off one of Bran's silver slippers. The
dog had always worn them in battle, and when he lashed
out with the freed paw, its claws pierced the black dog's
chest and punctured its heart.

'Bran killed my dog,' the stranger said to Conán, with
not a little wonder.

'Bran did, and now I'll do the same to you,' Conán
replied. He sliced off the stranger's head and placed it in
the puddle, in revenge for the disgrace he himself had
suffered. Everybody cheered him and, satisfied, he
resumed his doorkeeping duties.

A man arrived carrying a big trough of water. He
offered to wash the best man in the house and again Fionn
nominated Conán. Glad of the chance to cool down after
all the hot work fighting, Conán was about to jump in
when Fionn shouted a warning.

'Take your time! First, try the part of your body for
which you have least use.'

Despite some bawdy suggestions from his friends,
Conán selected one of his small toes. It burned to ashes
when it touched the water. Conán grabbed the stranger
and threw him into his own trough. He bubbled and
disintegrated. Then Conán threw the remainder of the
water over the six hundred sitting opposite the few of the

Fianna. All who were splashed melted away like beeswax
in a fire.

Conán's colleagues chastised him for all the intrusions,
but there were more to come. A small, thick-set man
arrived with a grey boar. When he threw it at the
doorstep, the house shook and those inside shuddered as
its supporting pillars tilted.

'Have that for your supper,' the man said, and ninety-
nine of those who had survived the water rushed to take
the boar to the kitchen. They could not move it an inch.
Conán suggested cooking it *in situ*. He piled firewood
around it, but when he lit it, the boar screeched and
pushed the fire and Conán through the door.

Outraged, Conán went to kill boar's owner. The man
begged for mercy and promised to cook the boar on four
golden spits. Conán sought Fionn's advice and agreed to
accept the offer. Man and beast disappeared. After a few
hours the man returned with four quarters perfectly
roasted on four golden spits.

Conán complained, 'Sure, Fionn eats at least one
forequarter. The other fifteen will require the other.
Normally we give the dogs a hindquarter; I know Bran is
the only one left, but he deserves it for his valour this
night. I have fought a bit too, so I will keep the last
quarter for myself. The rest of you can go and find your
own supper.'

The enemy chief, helped by his son, tried to grab the
last quarter. In the mêlée, Conán's meat-knife accidentally
beheaded the youth. Conán put the head in the puddle
also, and then sat down and ate his fill. Satisfied, he stood
at the door again and awaited more trouble.

It soon arrived. A host of surly men slouched up, but
Conán called Bran out and, both replenished with the

succulent boar, they had no trouble in disposing of the
opposition. The puddle was becoming full of heads, and
the enemy chief complained to Fionn about his inhospitable doorman. Fionn was replacing Conán with
Díarmuid when another stranger arrived carrying a huge
iron bar. Conán had a last fling — literally, for he caught
the stranger by the head and flung him. The head came
away in his hands and he added it to the pile in the puddle.

This was too much for the enemy leader. He
called what remained of his followers to take on the
sixteen Fianna.

Fionn rallied his men, telling them to stand shoulder
to shoulder and not let anyone pass.

The fight was furious. Showers of shield clippings,
sheets of sparks and pools of blood filled the refectory.
Then the stranger chief called for a truce until sunrise.
Fionn agreed.

When dawn broke, they went outside and continued
the battle. The gallant sixteen held their ground until
evening. Just as they began to weaken, the remainder of
the Fianna dashed from the surrounding woods, fresh and
eager for battle. They lashed out with unabated vigour
until every one of their opponents lay dead. Conán's
puddle could not hold half the enemy's heads. There was
no trace of the giant who had caused all the trouble, but
he never showed his face on the Hill of Allen or else-
where again.

SIX

The Salmon of Knowledge

Ireland's celebrated fishing rivers, the Boyne and the Shannon in particular, have their place in the country's mythology. Fionn Mac Cumhaill was celebrated for his great wisdom. One explanation for this claims that he entered the hill dwelling of the fairies and drank a draught from the Well of the Otherworld. Another tells how he caught his thumb in the door of a house in Sligo's Curlew Mountains or on Tipperary's Slievenamon. The door slammed, causing a goddess bearing a cup full of *don lionn iomhais* (liquid of inspiration) to stumble. Some of the vessel's contents splashed on Fionn's thumb and he put it into his mouth to soothe it.

The most popular account, however, has Fionn receiving his wisdom from the Salmon of Knowledge. No woman could ever catch this fish. One who tried, Sionnan, approached the Well of Connla in Cavan's Cuilcagh Mountains in which the salmon lived. She tried the poachers' belly-tickling method, but to no avail. The salmon splashed the water with fin and tail. So great was its strength that great streams formed from the displacement. Nine of these flowed beside Nine Sacred Hazels, racing in pursuit of the fleeing Sionnan. In doing so, they formed the great river Shannon. They overtook Sionnan, drowned her and cast her body into the Land of Mortals through a large hole, still reputed to have no bottom — Lug na Sionna, the river's source.

Now, in preparation for taking over leadership of the Fianna, Fionn learned a little sorcery from Bobdall and some swordsmanship from Luacha, two County Meath druidesses with whom he lived for a few years. His progress pleased them, but they knew they could never pass on wisdom to their charge because they were too ignorant. They consulted with a wise neighbour called Finegas and he agreed to be Fionn's tutor in the arts and sciences. The absent-minded Finegas never repaired the roof of his hut, seldom changed his clothes and forgot to eat, save when some Nuts of Wisdom fell from a magic tree nearby. These gave him great powers of inspiration, but could never equal that which would pass on to the first person to taste the flesh of the Salmon of Knowledge. At first he refused the women their request, but the nuts had given him the sense to realise that since he was growing old, the assistance of a strong young lad around the place would be useful. So he agreed.

For hours each day, the old man watched the Boyne flow past his holding. Fionn often noticed him lying on the bank with his eyes almost touching the water. The young trainee did not realise that his mentor was watching out for the Salmon of Knowledge (inquisitive people who question how the fish got from Cavan to Meath are told that they have not the wisdom to understand!).

On many previous occasions, Finegas had tried angling, but no matter what rod or line he used — even the stoutest hazel and the gut of a Drogheda cat — the salmon shattered it contemptuously, simply by flicking its tail. With Fionn helping to cook, mend and sew clothes and shoes, the old man spent even more time hunting the fish. Fionn was a good fisherman too, and one day he caught two prime specimens and began making a meal for Finegas. He cleaned out the fish and placed them on a spit above a fire. They sizzled away as Fionn prepared some garnishing. He hacked honey from a hive and ground fruit and nuts into it. The old man was very pleased. He was even more delighted when Fionn thatched his roof and repaired the walls of his cabin. The only thing that worried him was Fionn's skill at fishing, because he wanted the Salmon of Knowledge for himself.

Time passed and Finegas instructed his ward in painting, music and some less artistic sciences. Fionn absorbed all the knowledge, but Finegas never told him

how he could become the most learned man in the world.
One fine spring day, Finegas saw his prey stirring among
the weeds on the bed of the river. Hastily he assembled a
rod and line and selected a tempting bait. The Salmon of
Knowledge did not approach it, nor did any small trout,
so Finegas threw the whole apparatus into the water in
disgust. As he did, the fish poked its head above the water
and grinned.

'The Salmon! It's the Salmon of Knowledge!' the old
man shouted, and Fionn heard.

'Where? Where?' he yelled. The old man pointed.
Fionn saw nothing but a wash, just as a big boat would
leave. He remembered hearing something from Luacha
about the fish that had great powers but when he asked
Finegas to tell him more, the poet became sullen and
abrupt. He more or less told him to mind his own busi-
ness. The kindly Fionn went deep into the wood and
found a stout willow. He trimmed a strong, winding ivy
and fashioned it into a line. Then he prepared a comfort-
able seat beside the river, set Finegas upon it and placed
the rod in his frail hands. At the first cast, there was a
thundering splash. A bite! The salmon was pulling the old
man towards the Boyne. As the phantom fish sped
towards the opposite bank, it pulled Finegas into the
water. Fionn grabbed his legs and, using all his strength,
hauled Finegas and the salmon onto the bank. Huge silver
scales flashed in the sunlight, almost blinding the pair. The
fish whipped its tail in fury and felled an oak and an ash
with its lash. As it struggled for life, it burrowed a hole in
the bank that present-day archaeologists claim to be a
mediaeval passage tomb. Eventually its life ebbed away
and Fionn set about cleaning it out in preparation for a
banquet — because everyone in County Meath could

have dined well for a week on the fish.

Finegas forbad any immediate feasting, however. He said to Fionn, 'Eat all you like later on tonight, but I must be the first to taste the fish.'

The cooking took a long time. Fionn built a spit from the ash that the salmon had knocked down. He used its branches to build a huge fire beneath. The fish's size posed a problem. The heat needed to ensure that it was thoroughly roasted was intense. This caused large blisters to form on the skin. One of these rose above the bushes and Fionn prodded it with his thumb to burst it. He burned himself, and put thumb in his mouth to ease the pain. So Fionn became the first person to taste the Salmon of Knowledge.

Unaware of this, he made a huge platter from a shallow shale rock hewn from a nearby quarry. He placed a tempting pink steak on it and served it to Finegas. The old man looked into his pupil's eyes. We do not know what he saw, but he spoke in a soft, sad voice.

'Your eyes glow with wonder and they look beyond me. You have tasted the salmon.'

Fionn denied this, but explained about the blister and the thumb.

'There is no further need for you to be my pupil. I can teach you nothing more. You are now the wisest man in the world, so go from here.'

Fionn went with a heavy heart and Finegas pined away, sad to have missed his life's ambition, but serene in the knowledge that the Fianna would have a powerful and wise leader.

SEVEN

Fionn and the Scottish Giant

Visitors to the Giant's Causeway, near Bushmills in County Antrim, can see interesting rock formations. Geologists might explain how a cooling of lava in the Cainozoic Period brought about the phenomenon, but legend uses simpler language. It gives the groups of polygonal columns names like the Giant's Grandmother, the Giant's Chair and the Giant's Organ. Since there are traces of the formation at Staffa on Scotland's Isle of Skye, too, the ancient bards explained that mighty men of both races built the causeway across the sea to accommodate their mutual philandering.

Fionn Mac Cumhaill was feeling out of sorts one day. He was tired of swordfighting against inferiors and of wrestling men he could toss across his Allen fortress until they landed in Cork. Lying on a mossy bank, he threw stones to pass the time. They were not pebbles; some of them weighed a ton or more. He was facing east, so they fell in Dublin and the clever locals constructed a harbour with them.

Fionn was still bored, so he idled around, hoping to get a few of the Fianna to organise a hurling match. They were all away hunting, but he saw a small stranger coming towards him. This fellow ended Fionn's apathy. A messenger from Scotland, he said that one of that country's most feared fighters, Fear Ruadh, was on his way to challenge Fionn.

Everybody knew that this Red Man was a yard taller than Fionn, who himself towered over every man in Ireland. The prospect of their encounter excited Fionn, but he decided to be discreet. He sought his wife's advice and accepted it. Indeed, Gráinne directed events from that moment.

Fear Ruadh duly arrived. The stamp of his great feet made the ground tremble and Fionn heard their thud when Ruadh was passing through Kilcock, County Kildare. By the time he reached Robertstown, the din was almost unbearable. Fionn had to put five pounds of moss in each ear to dull it. Rapping on Fionn's door with a spear as long as the highest round tower in Ireland, the mighty visitor called out.

'Where is the great Irish giant they call Mac Cumhaill?'

'He is gone to Kerry to hunt deer,' a servant answered, 'but the woman of the house is within and will have a word with you.'

The servant ushered Fear Ruadh into the great hall of Allen. He pointed to articles that the astute Gráinne had hastily assembled there.

'There's the master's spear.' It was a straight fir tree, with a long pointed stone at its top.

'Over there is Fionn's shield.' The Scottish giant saw a block hewn from the greatest oak in Ireland. It was as big as four carriage-wheels and was rimmed with an iron hoop six inches wide.

'Well, I'll be hanged!' exclaimed Fear Ruadh in amazement.

When Gráinne entered, she graciously invited the visitor to sit for a meal, apologising for the fact that she had only their everyday fare to offer. She placed a cake of griddle-bread in front of him. Fear Ruadh was hungry after his long journey, so he bit hard into it. This broke three of his teeth, because Gráinne had left the iron griddle inside the cake.

She had been more ingenious with the meat. This was just a strip of hard fat nailed to the rim of a block of red deal. When the giant tried to bite into this, he smashed another molar or two. As he attempted to hide his pain, Gráinne casually broke a piece off the bread. In the making, she had ensured that this piece covered the hole that formed the griddle handle. She gave the helping to the baby in the cradle, who devoured it before winking at the visitor playfully. The baby was Fionn himself, attired in dress and bonnet.

Filled with apprehension, Fear Ruadh was having second thoughts about challenging Fionn to combat.

Gráinne next placed a five-gallon bucket of honey beer before the giant. A little upset by the bad food, he drank this in one gulp. The servant brought him outside for a walk. Fear Ruadh asked how the Fianna amused themselves and the lad pointed to six huge boulders, each as big as a gatepost.

'These are finger stones that they toss around, sometimes as far as Cork,' the youth said. He explained that some of the rocks stuck in the earth and could be seen in many places around Ireland. Fear Ruadh tried his hand, whirling a boulder around his head and letting it fly. It landed almost a mile away.

'Not bad!' the servant remarked. 'When you grow a bit and train with the Fianna, you'll do better.'

The giant asked about other pastimes and the youth showed him a huge round boulder, saying, 'Fionn and the lads throw that across the castle, then run around the moat and catch it before it lands. Try it!'

Fear Ruadh had difficulty even lifting the rock. When he raised it above his head, it slipped and fell on his neck, thus giving him only a slight twinge of pain, because the skull of a Scotsman is very hard. If it is, the head is full of sense, however, because Fear Ruadh said he would not wait around for Fionn's return. He asked the servant to give his thanks to Gráinne and to tell her that he had to reach Scotland before the tide came in.

Off he went, full of wonderment at the great men who lived in Ireland. Fionn jumped out of the cradle and hugged Gráinne. He thanked her, saying that women should be given more power because they were so shrewd. Just to give the giant another fright, he took off after him. Fear Ruadh had made good ground, however and was halfway across the sea when Fionn passed Portadown in County Armagh. Mac Cumhaill tore a sod of earth from the ground and flung it after Fear Ruadh. The wind took it off course and it splashed harmlessly in the sea miles south of its target. Today, they call it the Isle of Man. The hole left in the earth filled up with water and formed what is now Lough Neagh.

EIGHT

The Persecution of Étain

L one green hills, often topped by a single bushy-top tree, can be seen in many places in Ireland. Mounds that archaeologists regard as burial places of royal personages are more often called 'fairy forts' or 'fairy raths' by country people. When defeated by the Milesians, the Tuatha Dé Danaan retired to these places, where they built great castles and palaces. Occasionally they emerged in some human form, perhaps to woo young women with whom they had become infatuated. Such was the case in the legend of the god Midir Mórálach (Proud Midir) and Étain, who was daughter of King Ailill from Echraidhe in Ulster (not to be confused with other Ailills).

Midir lived in Brí Leith, Sliabh gCállraighe (Golry, now known as the Hill of Ardagh) in County Longford. He was the foster-father of Aengus Óg, the god of love. Étain was known in every town and village in Ireland for her great beauty, and Midir lusted for her. Midir's wife, Fuamnach, became suspicious at his being away so much. So closely did she watch him that he had to enlist the aid of Aengus Óg in his clandestine courtship. Aengus organised the arrangements with Étain's father, who made heavy demands. First Ailill forced him to clear twelve great land-tracts of tree and shrub. Then he ordered him to divert twelve rivers to flow through them for drainage. Finally, Ailill demanded Étain's weight in gold and silver.

When Aengus complied with these requirements, Midir claimed his bride and brought her back to Longford. Fuamnach became insanely jealous. She had certain evil powers herself, but to make sure of a successful

spell, she asked a druid to help her. Between them they
managed to turn Étain into a pool of water. In this, her
own substance, she became a maggot which in time
matured into a magnificent crimson butterfly. All these
transformations were designed to confuse.

The butterfly could make haunting music which
Midir loved, so Fuamnach arranged for a great storm that
blew it out to sea, and then back across the land. It
managed, however, to settle on Aengus's chest as he lay
dozing in the sun at Brúgh na Bóinne (Brugh of Boyne).

It should be said that the god of love always diplayed
his kisses in a halo of blue birds that fluttered around his
head. He may have helped his foster-father to win Étain,
but he was not one to shun good female company and so
he built a gazebo of the finest crystal for the butterfly. He
placed sweet-smelling flowers and shrubs in it and
arranged that the spell would be effective only during
daylight hours, so he would have the pleasure of Étain's
company by night.

A few years later, Fuamnach found out about this and
arranged for a more lasting storm. For a thousand years it
blew the butterfly hither and thither. During that time,
Midir roamed the country in search of Étain in human
form, because he knew nothing of the enchantment. One
night Etar, the King of Leinster, was dining with influen-
tial friends. The wind blew the butterfly into the refectory
and, blinded by the light, it clung to a rafter above the top
table. Tired from years of hardship, it dozed and fell into
the queen's golden *meidir* (drinking-cup). When she
drank, she swallowed the butterfly and became pregnant.
She gave birth nine months later. The infant was Étain,
now reborn in human form but unaware of her past. Fate
took a hand and she retained her original name.

The new Étain grew up to be incredibly beautiful. A bachelor king, Eochaidh Airemh, ruled at Tara and his henchmen were pressing him to marry. They disliked bringing their own wives to the palace entertainments, knowing that the king could order their submission to him if the fancy took him. They recommended the lovely Étain as a bride. One day the king was out hunting. He came across a group of young women lying in a meadow. The white flesh of one — Étain — shone in the sunlight and Eochaidh fell hopelessly in love with her. After a short courtship, they married and lived at Tara.

Étain was a popular hostess. During one of the great assemblies at the royal residence, she moved among the chieftains and warriors, exchanging pleasantries and encouraging them at their games. Then she saw a white horse charging across the plain. A handsome rider in regal robes reined it in. It was Midir, but she remembered nothing of their former association. He asked her to come away with him to Tír na nÓg, the Land of Eternal Youth, but she said, 'I cannot go without my husband's consent.' Midir knew the king would never give that, so he rode away, disconcerted.

However, he thought of a plan and a few months later returned to put it into effect. After meeting Eochaidh, he challenged him to play ficheall, a game like chess. Using a confidence ruse like today's three-card-tricksters, Midir allowed the king to win the first two games and he paid his forfeit willingly. He then suggested a game for which the winner would declare the loser's forfeit. Midir won and demanded a hug and a kiss from Étain. 'Damn your impertinence,' shouted Eochaidh. 'Come back next month and you will receive them.'

While Midir was gone, Étain's love for him reawoke.

She pined and longed for the time agreed upon for the kiss. As that day neared, she was distraught when she saw Eochaidh assembling his troops around the castle to prevent her lover's entry. This made little difference to a god, however, and Midir suddenly appeared beside her. They embraced and kissed and friendly gods spirited them up through the roof. Then they turned into two white swans and flew away.

For over a year, Eochaidh searched for them. He dug up fairy raths and watched in woodland glades where the *sidhe* (fairies) played their hurling matches and ran races. There was no sign of the elopers. He raided Brí Leith, where he heard Midir's voice telling him that Étain would return to him the following day. Exactly on the third hour, the appointed time, fifty young women, all resembling Étain, appeared in the High King's ante-chamber. Étain was one of them, but Eochaidh did not choose her. It was their daughter, Étain Óg, whom he selected. Tragically, they slept together and begot a child, another girl, who grew up and married Cormac, king of Ulster. Their first-born was a girl, but Cormac wanted a boy, so he threw the unfortunate infant into a pit. This trend continued, tragedy following every union of a descendant of Étain.

When Bódearg succeeded Dagda as leader of the Túatha Dé Danaan, Midir refused to accept him. He enlisted the aid of Fionn Mac Cumhaill and the Fianna to challenge Bódearg. This war lasted for years and marked the final withdrawal of the Tuatha Dé Danaan to the safety of their Irish hills, deep in the earth and far removed from jealous and vindictive mortals. There, Midir still mourned the loss of Étain, and some people say that the sighing breezes that whisper through those lone trees on Irish hills are the echoes of his weeping.

NINE

Déirdre of the Sorrows and the Sons of Uisneach

The Hill of Uisneach, near Ballymore, County Westmeath, has a large 'catstone', so called because, viewed from beneath, it looks like a giant cat. Some geographers regarded this rock, Ail na Mireann (Stone of Divisions), as the navel or centre of Ireland. The five ancient provinces of Ireland converged there. Although there is no evidence of any association, the father of famous sons in mythology bears the same name.

Scholars claim that the Third Sorrow of Storytelling, the Exile of the Sons of Uisneach (*Oidhe Cloinne Uisneach*), contributed to the establishment of the Romantic movement in European literature. It begins during Cuchullain's golden years as hero of the Red Branch Knights (*Ridirí Craobh Ruadh*). This corps of warriors guarded Ulster during the reign of King Conor Mac Nessa. One evening, Conor and his men were feasting at the home of the royal *seanchaí*, Fedlimid. As the entertainment continued, Fedlimid's wife gave birth to a girl. The druid, Cathbad, announced that he had heard this infant crying from her mother's womb and that she would grow to be a beautiful woman for whom men would fight. She would bring ruin upon Ulster, he predicted. Some warriors wanted her killed there and then, but the King promised to foster her and hide her away from all eyes but his own. 'I will wed her myself when she matures,' he said.

Gale-force winds and torrential rain followed the birth and caused great floods. Those present did not worry about this because Fedlimid's cellar and table were good.

The waters subsided and Conor returned to his seat at
Eamhain Macha, near Armagh, with the infant, whom he
called Déirdre. Close by, in a remote part of the country,
his governess, Leabharcham, took charge and succeeded in
raising the child. The only time she saw other mortals was
when Leabharcham allowed her to peep through the
trees to watch the Red Branch Knights play hurling.
On one of these occasions a particular athlete impressed
Déirdre considerably.

When she turned seventeen, Déirdre had long raven-
black hair, cheeks blushed like a wild rose and a graceful
body. Overcome by her beauty, Conor Mac Nessa
became even more intent on keeping her concealed; he
wanted to make sure she would be his alone.

One day the king killed a calf and began skinning it
in the snow outside Leabharcham's house. A raven
alighted and began pecking at the carcass until blood
spilled out. Déirdre was watching through the window.
The governess heard her whisper, 'One day I will marry
a man like that. He will have raven-black hair, a snow-
white body and blood-red cheeks; a man like the one I
noticed hurling.'

Leabharcham questioned her charge and came to the
conclusion that she was speaking about Naoise, one of the
three sons of Uisneach. He, Ainle and Ardan were famous
for their skill in arms, for wrestling, running and chariot-
racing. They were brave and fearless. Their mother,
Ebhla, was the daughter of Cathbad the druid, who had
made the post-natal predictions about Déirdre.

Accounts differ about what happened next. Some say
Leabharcham became an accomplice, others that Déirdre
took to walking the woods and plains around the camps of
the Red Branch Knights. In any event, the pair met and fell

in love. With his brothers and other warriors acting as
bodyguards, Naoise carried Déirdre away from Ulster. Just
like Díarmuid and Gráinne, they roamed from kingdom to
kingdom, never able to rest properly in any one place
because Conor and his army were in pursuit. Eventually the
brothers advised their loyal comrades to return to Conor
and plead forgiveness. They themselves took Déirdre to
Alba (Scotland) and settled near a lake called Etiebh.

The brothers hunted by day and, because they were
faster runners than any Scotsman, they caught the choicest
deer and the sweetest rabbits. Each evening Déirdre
cooked a sumptuous meal and they ate heartily. They
drank their fill, too, because they had given allegiance to
the King of Alba and he plied them with the finest wines
and his famous heather-beer.

Readers often wonder if Ainle and Ardan were
jealous of Naoise or if they resented their exile on his
behalf. This was not so; an incredibly close brotherly love
united them. However, they did miss battles they had
once fought in Ireland, so they built a castle for Déirdre at
Oileán na Rón (Seal Island) and went to war against the
clans of Alba. They won a few small kingdoms, but meanwhile the King of Alba had heard about Déirdre's beauty
and was making plans to have her for himself.

Although madly in love with Naoise, Déirdre's vanity
led her to feign interest in the King's overtures. One day
she was playing chess with Naoise. He had just returned
from a battle and was a little homesick, because the Scottish
opposition did not really test him. Déirdre won the game
and teasingly gloated about it. Naoise stood up abruptly and
said, 'What man minds losing a silly game when everything
he cares about is lost.' Then Déirdre realised how much
her man missed Ireland and she grew worried.

Perhaps it was female intuition because, without knowing it, she had reason for concern. Word had reached King Conor about the Scottish king's amorous intent. He was furious, so he sent Cuchullain and two other gallant fighters, Fergus McRoth and Conal Cearnach, to Scotland to bring Déirdre home. He told them he was granting the sons of Uisneach a pardon and that they would be safe if they returned to Ireland. This was not his intent. He still wanted Déirdre for himself and wished to punish her escorts.

Just after the chess game, Déirdre heard someone shout out in an Irish brogue. The sound alerted Naoise, but she tried to persuade him that it was the accent of a Scotsman with too much drink in him. Ardan followed the sound and met the three Red Branch Knights. He brought them to the castle and there was a great party that night. There was another the evening before they all left Alba. The second was spoiled when Déirdre recounted a dream. In it, three ravens flew out of the seat of the Ulster kings, Eamhain Macha, and reached Etiebh. Each carried in its beak a sprig of a yew tree, a death symbol. Upon these were drops of honey, which they placed in the mouths of the three sons of Uisneach and Déirdre. Then they pecked drops of blood from each, to replace the honey. The significance was obvious, but the men laughed and ignored the portent. Furthermore, Fergus promised to defend the sons of Uisneach against all comers. Déirdre sang a lament for Scotland, a country she had grown to love, and they all set sail for Ireland.

King Conor had arranged a diversion. He encouraged relatives of the returned exiles to meet them when their ship docked at Drogheda, County Meath. The Red Branch Knights had a rule forbidding them to refuse a feast and, as soon as the party landed, there was an invitation for Fergus McRoth alone to attend one. He had pledged his protection to the others, so, to get over his dilemma, he appointed his sons, Red Buinne the Ruthless and Iollan the Fair, to deputise for him on the journey to Eamhain Macha. This offended the sons of Uisneach.

Déirdre became alarmed when she saw a nimbus of blood around her lover's head. She begged Naoise to go with her to Cuchullain's home in Dundalk, but he refused.

Before they reached their destination, they met Leabharcham, who cried when she saw that the girl she had reared was as beautiful as ever. She took her away to hide her again, sending word to Conor that Déirdre was now old and ugly and no fit match for a king.

Meanwhile the sons of Uisneach wined and dined with Conor. After that, Ainle and Ardan remained at the fortress for a few days, but Naoise went to Déirdre's hiding-place. Conor ordered a spy called Trendhorn to track them down and report to him. This fellow found Leabharcham's hovel, but its doors and windows were closed and shuttered. Nevertheless, he found a tiny window under the thatch and climbed up and peeped through it. Naoise and Déirdre were playing chess inside and Naoise was becoming bored at the lack of opposition. He leaned back in his chair, yawning, and saw the eye of the spy peering in. Grabbing the nearest chess-piece, a bishop, he hurled it with all his force at the window. It blasted Trendhorn's eye from its socket. The spy returned to Conor, swearing he would sacrifice one eye any day for a peep at the beautiful Déirdre.

A furious Conor now prepared for all-out revenge. He sent fifty soldiers to kill the sons of Uisneach but, with

Fergus's sons in support, they survived the assault. The king tried burning them out, but again he was unsuccessful. An attack by his son Fiachra with his enchanted shield failed, as did another armed attack. Then Conor resorted to sorcery. His druids led the sons into a forest of enchanted trees, but they found their way through it easily. They spirited Déirdre and the men into a raging sea, but Naoise took his woman on his back and held her safely while the others enjoyed a swim. A third spell turned the sea into ice, which hacked at the flesh when the men tried to cut their way out of it.

Some versions of the sons' fate claim that they froze to death in this sea of ice. They have a moving sequel: Déirdre leaps into Naoise's grave and clings to him before dying of a broken heart. Others tell how the men finally fell in battle. One poignant account claims that the three were surrounded and were about to be executed by Red-fisted Maine, son of the King of Norway — called in because no Ulsterman would do the dirty deed. At the last minute, Naoise took his sword, bestowed on him by the sea-god Manannan Mac Lir, gave it to Maine, and then placed his neck alongside his brothers'. All three died by a single slash.

When the Red Branch Knights buried the sons of Uisneach, Fergus deserted in disgust and joined the army of the King of Connaght, while Conor Mac Nessa forced Déirdre to live with him. She remained frigid and aloof, telling him that she hated the sight of him. She also loathed Eoghan, son of Durtacht; this henchman had helped to kill her lover and his brothers.

Leering maliciously, Conor said, 'Well, if you will not sleep with me, I will order Eoghan to rape you,' and he began making arrangements for her to move to her enemy's house.

Déirdre was distraught. She ran into the fields and
battered her head against a large rock until she was dead.
Ever since, sympathetic chroniclers have called her
'Déirdre of the Sorrows'.

TEN

Fionn and the Daughter of the King of Greece

County Kerry was a favourite recreation area for legendary Irish characters. One day Fionn and the Fianna were hunting on the lower slopes of Mount Brandon, on the Dingle peninsula. They saw a ship heading for the shore. Dashing down excitedly, they noticed that there was nobody on board except a woman. A woman at sea was considered unlucky, but they ignored superstition and welcomed her ashore.

The woman challenged Fionn to a game of forfeits. He agreed and won the first game. For his prize, he demanded a white horse with a red saddle for each of his men. She obliged. The woman won the next game and placed her opponent under *geasa* (a binding injunction) to marry her and live as her husband until seven shovels of earth covered his head. Although Fionn had no option but to comply, he ordered his men to stand guard on the mountains around the coast while he was away. Then he embarked and set sail with the woman.

As soon as they had left, the horses and saddles evaporated from under the Fianna. The couple reached Greece. When they landed, the woman told Fionn how to reach her father's castle by a circuitous route. She herself sped ahead and got her father to send out men to meet and capture Fionn. They did so, and then cast the Irish chieftain in prison, heavily bound.

After many months, Fionn asked permission to go out into the garden with one arm loosened. His request was granted. Once outside, Fionn whipped his *barrabuadh* (horn) from his waistband and blew a loud blast on it. Standing on a lone peak in Kerry, Díarmuid heard and knew his master was in need of help. He covered seven acres of land in one jump and landed on the shore. Boarding a battered and abandoned craft, Díarmuid set sail.

On reaching Greece, he rushed to the palace and arrived just as his captors were about to burn Fionn at a stake. He roared at them to stop and challenged them to fight. Over two thousand volunteered, but Díarmuid called for as many more. He hacked his way through them and made neat piles of heads, bodies and weapons. Díarmuid was hungry after his long journey and his short fight. He demanded food and the Greek king sent him to his Hooligan's House (*Tigh na nAmhas*), where man-eating undesirables lived.

When he entered, the king locked the doors on him. Díarmuid killed all the inhabitants except the master of the house or chief *Amhas*, who submitted and became his servant. He told the ravenous Irishman that there was no food. Díarmuid went to the baker and demanded bread. Fearing the king, the baker refused, so Díarmuid pushed him into his oven and took away all the loaves he could carry. Likewise the wine-merchant; when he refused, Díarmuid shoved him head first into a cask of wine before taking three casks for himself.

Díarmuid and the chief *Amhas* ate and drank for four hours. They sang and danced for another four and rested for the remainder of the night. The hot eastern sun woke Díarmuid early. He arose, went outside and called for more fighting. Because they had witnessed his prowess the previous day, most of the king's men were hiding. The king ordered any who, foolishly, were still

hanging around to take on the Irishman. Díarmuid
disposed of them quickly.

On his third day in Greece, Díarmuid demanded
battle or Fionn's release. The stubborn king said, 'You
cannot see Fionn until you bring me the Hound and the
Gold Chain from *Caol an Iarainn* (Iron Caol).'

'Where will I find them?' Díarmuid asked.

'I will not tell you. Search for yourself,' the king
answered impudently, considering his loss of an army.

The chief *Amhas* had become very friendly at this
stage and he guided Díarmuid to Caol's castle.

'There it is, built on a small piece of land that revolves.'

Díarmuid watched the edifice turn and noticed a
single small window very high up. When it came around
again, he took a leap and succeeded in climbing through
the opening. Caol was asleep, so Díarmuid had no trouble
getting away with the Hound and the Gold Chain.
Halfway back to the castle, however, he had a pang of
conscience, feeling it improper that a member of the
Fianna should have committed an act that amounted to
theft, and in a foreign country. Returning, he roused
Caol and told him why he had come.

'If you do not hand them over willingly, I must fight
you for them,' Díarmuid said.

Caol turned on his heel without saying a word. He
went into another room and returned with two swords.
Throwing them on the ground, he said, 'Select one.'

'They are both the same,' Díarmuid replied. He took
one and handed the other to Caol.

All day they fought, like two raging lions or two mad
bulls or two wild boars. They made soft ground hard and
hard ground soft with their stamping and jumping. By
evening, they had worn a number of swords to the hilt.

Caol got two more and they fought on into the night. Again, the swords were worn out. Caol suggested getting another pair, but Díarmuid shouted that he would fight without a weapon. With that, he seized Caol by the neck and thighs and broke his back over his knee, as he would a twig. Caol was quite placid about this, merely asking Díarmuid to bring him to a healing spring nearby. 'If you do, I will give you the Hound and the Gold Chain,' he promised.

Díarmuid threw Caol over his back and, raising him so that he could give directions, set off. They came to the well and Caol said, 'Throw me down into it now and I'll be as fit as ever I was.' Díarmuid obliged, and the remedy worked. Caol kept his word and handed over the Hound and Gold Chain. Díarmuid rushed back to the King of Greece with them and demanded to see Fionn Mac Cumhaill. The monarch was not as honest as Caol. He refused, demanding that Díarmuid bring him in addition the Sword of Light and the *Fios Fátha an Doimhin-Scéil* (the Mystic Knowledge of the Deep Story — that is to say, the tasks performed in order to locate it).

Being used to honourable dealings, Díarmuid flew into a rage. He jumped up to a window at the top of the castle, entered and grabbed the king by the two feet and dashed him against the wall. He turned threateningly to the household and warned, 'Every one of you will get the same treatment if you do not show me to my master.'

They rushed to help and soon Diarmuid was embracing a delighted prisoner. As he laughed, Fionn's mouth fell open so wide that Díarmuid saw his heart and his liver. The pair rushed back to the vessel and set sail. Bad as the boat was, they were soon cruising along the south-west coast of Ireland. When they were passing Slea Head, Fionn became anxious.

'The daughter of the King of Greece is full of magic and wicked spells,' he said to Díarmuid. 'Climb to the crow's nest and look south and west in case she is following.'

Up went Díarmuid and, sure enough, he spotted the daughter in the distance. She had adopted the form of a crow, but that did not fool Díarmuid. He slid back down the mast and began steering the ship towards the shore. Fionn was still uneasy and told Díarmuid to climb up and have another look. This time the crow-princess was much nearer.

They were then close to Ballyferriter. 'Quickly! Jump onto the shore,' Díarmuid shouted. Fionn leaped and Díarmuid followed. They were just in time, for the enchanted crow set fire to their ship. She then took on her true form and faced Díarmuid.

'Why did you take my husband away from me, you long speckle-shinned woman's man?' she screamed.

'What right have you to call him your husband,' challenged Díarmuid.

'Every right,' she said. 'He is under *geasa* to me until seven shovels of earth cover his head.'

'Very well,' Díarmuid laughed, then dug a grave and placed Fionn in it. Covering him with seven shovels of clay, he said, 'Now you own him no longer, but you can take him.'

She bent down to lift Fionn and Díarmuid hit her a fierce blow on the head with the shovel, killing her. Then he scraped the soil from Fionn.

They both cast the body of the daughter of the King of Greece into the sea. Legend says her head is now a large rock, the best on the coast of Kerry for shellfish.

ELEVEN

The Origin of Irish Cattle

Two islands, one off the Galway coast, the other off Donegal, bear the name Inishbofin. Bó Finn means white cow. One legend tells how the Galway island was enchanted and appeared in the sea only at odd intervals. One day two fishermen landed there and lit a fire to roast some fish. This broke the enchantment and the island remained. Next they saw an old woman driving a white cow along the shingle. She struck the beast and it turned into a rock. The men abused her and slapped her face, whereupon they too turned to stone.

A more profitable tale links the island with the origin of Ireland's fine beef. A beautiful girl rose out of the sea one day. She drove three strange-looking beasts on to the shore. They were the sacred cows Bó Finn, Bó Dubh and Bó Dearg (white, black and red cows). The red cow headed for Ulster and the black one for Munster. Bó Finn, however, had loftier aspirations and a mind for good grazing land. She set off for Tara of the Kings in County Meath. There she produced a male and female calf, from which came a royal herd. Her work done, she returned to the shore, where she entered a deep cave to rest. She still sleeps there and will not re-emerge until a worthy king rules again in Ireland, finds her and rouses her.

TWELVE

The Sons of Tuireann

The families of Donegal fishermen believed that tragedy could befall seafarers if an enemy uttered an incantation while pointing certain stones on Tory Island in the direction of their vessel. Islanders called these 'The Cursing Stones of Tory'. A greater evil once existed on the island: an ogre who was dreaded throughout the land. He plays a prominent role in the First Sorrow of Storytelling, the Fate of the Sons of Tuireann.

The Formorians were a savage pirate race who often raided the Tuatha Dé Danaan, stole their cattle and property and imposed levies on them. Taxes were levied on grinding stones and other paraphernalia for making bread.

Balor of the Evil Eye was the most dreaded of all the Formorians. This giant was the god of death. Ugly and coarse, he had only one eye. Anybody who looked at it died instantly. As he grew older, a horrible leathery lid grew over this eye and his colleagues had to fit a block and tackle for raising it when they wished to kill an enemy. No weapon could slay the giant, but a sorceress told him that his grandson would cause his demise. He therefore locked his only child, Eithlinn, in a round tower on Tory Island to prevent her conceiving.

A son of the medicine god, Dian Cécht, heard of this girl's beauty. His enchanted cow, Glasgamhan (Green calf), had been on the island since the Formorians' last raid, so he daringly dressed as a cow-woman to gain access to the Tory estate and retrieve the animal. He also found time to sleep with Eithlinn. She gave birth to Lugh. Balor cast the infant into the sea, but Manannan Mac Lir, the sea-god (some say Goibniu, the smithgod), fostered him and he grew up to be the famous Lugh an Láimh Fada (Lugh of the Long Arm), who gave his name to the great harvest festival of Lughnasa. This sun-god travelled in an amphibious craft belonging to his foster-father. Named *The Sweeper*, it did not depend on wind-direction, but went wherever its master wished. Lugh carried a sword that could slice through an iron bar as if it was butter. He called it *An Freagróir* (The Answerer).

The handsome young warrior became the talk of the land. A subdued and oppressed race perked up a little, hoping that with his help they might yet defeat the Formorians. Their hero-worship was so great that they called the Milky Way 'Lugh's Chain' and the rainbow 'Lugh's Sling'. They were right. When tax-paying time came around again, the druid-king Nuada and his followers assembled on the Hill of Uisneach. They saw Balor's avaricious collectors approaching from the north. Another crowd was coming from the south. Lugh was at their head. A radiant light shone from his face and from his white steed. Nuada's company stood and bowed to Balor's men, whereupon Lugh chastised them for not treating him with similar respect. Then he set upon Balor's collectors and dispersed them. The incident provoked outright war between the Tuatha Dé Danaan and the Formorians.

As Lugh marched towards Tara, mustering the fairy folk from their hill-keeps, his father, Cian, went north to enlist the aid of the men of Ulster. When crossing Mámuirthemne (the Plain of Muirthemne) between the river Boyne and Dundalk, he met Brian, Iucharbha and Iuchar, the sons of Tuireann and the goddess Brigid. They were his enemies.

It was important not to delay, so, to avoid any encounter, Cian touched himself with his druidic wand, whereupon he became a pig. He tried to hide in a herd that was moving northward. Brian too used some sorcery. He turned his brothers into hounds and they separated the enchanted pig from the others. Brian then stabbed the animal with his spear. As it lay wounded, it spoke in a human voice, asking that human form should be restored. Brian complied and Cian then threatened that if he were finished off, his son Lugh of the Long Arm would exact revenge. Iuchar and Iucharba also returned to their human form and the three sons of Tuireann asked Cian how Lugh would know if they were to kill him.

'The weapons you use for the deed will cry out your guilt,' he replied.

'Then we shall stone you to death,' Brian shouted, and they did.

The three young men tried to bury the body, but the earth kept falling off it. They tried piling stones on top, but the same thing happened. After six attempts, they managed to bury the corpse in a deep trench.

Meanwhile, Lugh and his men had routed the Formorians. After a short rest, Lugh wondered what had become of his father, so he set out to look for him. When he passed the spot where Cian was buried, the body called from its grave, 'Your father lies here, slain by the sons of Tuireann. Revenge! Exact revenge!'

Lugh tore at the earth. When he looked on his father's battered body, he flew into a fierce rage. He rushed to Tara where King Nuadha was celebrating the victory over the Formorians. Lugh dashed into the refectory and denounced the killers, who were all present.

Nuadha thought the crime should be avenged by
lopping off one limb of each son every day until they died
from loss of blood, but Lugh was less barbarous. He
announced that, since the sons of Tuireann were members
of the victorious Tuatha Dé Danaan, he would accept a
fine of three apples, seven pigs and one pigskin, a spear,

a chariot and pair, a young dog, a cooking-spit, and three
shouts from a hill.

The culprits were overcome by this apparent
generosity. Ecstasy at its triviality gave way to terror,
however, when Lugh elaborated. The apples were the
fabled golden fruit from the Garden of the Sun in the
Eastern World. The seven pigs were the enchanted swine
of King Asal of the Golden Pillars in Egypt; no matter
how often these were slaughtered and eaten, they
reappeared, so they provided sustenance forever.
Furthermore, they provided a cure for many ills. The
King of Greece owned the pigskin. It too could cure
diseases and wounds.

King Pisar of Persia owned the spear. Its head was
always kept in water because it was so fiery and battle-
ready that it could burn down its owner's palace. Dobar,
King of Sicily, owned the chariot whose pair of horses
had no equals for fleetness. All the beasts in the world
would cringe before the bark of the King of Norway's
young bitch, Fáilinish (Island of Destiny). The spit
belonged to the women of an island beneath the sea
called Finchory.

The three shouts, on the surface derisory, became the
most formidable of Lugh's demands. They were to be
uttered from the Hill of Midcain in north Denmark.
Midcain was a celebrated fighter. He and his sons
defended that tor and Cian had been a great friend of
theirs. 'If I was easy on you for killing my father,' Lugh
said, 'they will not show you any mercy.'

On the advice of their father, Brian, Iuchar and
Iucharba borrowed Manannan Mac Lir's boat, *The
Sweeper*. His brothers wanted to fight for everything that
was demanded, but Brian urged prudence. They got the

apples by changing themselves into hawks, flying over the Garden of the Sun until its guardians had fired all their arrows and spears at them, and then diving for the fruit. They were pursued, but turned themselves into swans and swam under the water and back to their craft.

Knowing the Greeks' love of the arts, they arranged their hair and dress like poets in their quest for the pigskin. They composed some verses about the famed leather and recited them for the King. He was pleased, because he had never heard an Irish poem before. He asked what he could do for them and they replied 'Give us the pigskin.' The King refused, but he offered the next best thing: all the gold that the skin would hold. While servants measured out the ingots, Brian drew his sword and snatched the skin from the chancellor's assistants. He upbraided the King for thinking so little of Irish poetry, and then slew him. A fight ensued and the brothers were badly wounded. They fled to *The Sweeper* and covered themselves with the magic pelt, which healed them.

Their success prompted them to compose a better poem. They recited this to the King of Persia. It extolled his spear so extravagantly that they thought he would give it to them. When Pisar refused, Brian threw one of the golden apples at him and knocked him over. Then he rushed past the guards and grabbed the fiery spear. With this in his possession, the king's men were no match for the sons of Tuireann, who soon sailed for Sicily. There they joined Dobar's army and the king became greatly impressed by their fighting prowess. They never laid eyes on the chariot and pair, so they decided to complain. They said they felt hurt at not being trusted and wished to leave the army. Dobar held a parade. As the chariot neared, he boasted to the sons of Tuireann, 'These horses can gallop on land and on sea. Their speed has never been equalled. The chariot is inlaid with the world's most expensive jewels and miniature paintings.'

Like all proud men, Docar was extremely vain. When the chariot passed, he did not even notice Brian jumping into it and hurling out the charioteer. Iuchar lashed around him with the fiery spear from Persia. Iucharbar grabbed the reins and soon the sons were cantering on the wave crests to *The Sweeper*.

Word of their brave deeds spread and they got the pigs from King Asal without a struggle. Furthermore, he mediated with the King of Norway, who happened to be his son-in-law. The monarch would not give up the hound without a struggle, however, and there was a bloody battle, which the sons of Tuireann won.

Back home, Lugh heard of their successes. There were two steps to go to pay the fine in full, but the three had been away a long time and he wished to avail of the magic goods they had won to date. Therefore he placed a spell of forgetfulness upon them and, thinking they had achieved all their aims, they returned to Ireland. They were delighted to see their native shore again. Disembarking at Drogheda, they hurried to Tara in the enchanted chariot and gave it and the other prizes to Lugh. He accepted them gladly, but then pointed out that they still had two things to do before they would be free.

With heavy hearts they set off again. They endured three months of storm on board *The Sweeper* before Brian decided to dive in search of the submarine island of Finchory. He found it — a pleasant land full of comely seamstresses, who giggled at his boldness and his Irish roguishness. Like many women before them, they were overcome by the lad's charm and flattery. Although they

could easily have prevented it, they allowed him to take
the spit and leave. The sons then set sail to face their
last ordeal.

Midcain stood guard over his hill and refused Brian's
request to let him shout from it. The two men fought
long and hard and Brian eventually killed Midcain. The
victim's two sons rushed out. Some say it was the blood-
iest battle ever fought; the soil became drenched in blood
and each man suffered wounds through which a rat could
run. Eventually Midcain's three sons were killed, but the
sons of Tuireann were barely able to struggle to the hilltop
and emit a weak call. Brian had to carry his brothers back
to *The Sweeper*. All three lay down in the craft and it
steered itself back towards Ireland. They were extremely
weak and did not know what was happening. One day
Brian heard a gull call. He pulled himself up and saw the
crest of Howth Head in County Dublin. Farther on, he
smelt the rich pastureland of Meath.

Instead of docking in the Boyne estuary, Brian faced
the amphibious ship towards his father's mansion. When
he reached it, he told Tuireann to bring the spit to Lugh
at Tara and to tell him that they had shouted from the Hill
of Midcain, thus complying fully with his demands. Since
he and his brothers were almost dead, he asked his father
to request the loan of the healing pigskin that they had
brought from Greece. The old man delivered the spit and
the request, but Lugh refused to part with the pigskin.
Crestfallen, Tuireann returned and told Brian of Lugh's
meanness. Weary and beaten from the years of effort,
Brian lay down between his two brothers and moaned. All
three died at the same time and Tuireann knelt and wept
over their bodies. He kissed each one and fell dead on top
of them, his heart broken from grief.

THIRTEEN

Cuchullain's Death

Visitors to the General Post Office in Dublin's
O'Connell Street will notice a statue in bronze by
Oliver Sheppard. A memorial to the 1916 Rising, it
depicts the dying Cuchullain with a black raven on his
shoulder. Mythology contains a number of accounts of the
death of the great Red Branch Knight. Two of the most
popular are worth retelling.

The goddess of battle, the Morrígan, had many
encounters with Cuchullain. In these, she adopted various
guises. She became a heifer, an eel, a wolf and an old
woman milking a cow, but he fought her off every time.
Eventually she appeared to him as a beautiful woman and
craved his love. This was typical of her volatile attitude to
the hero — sometimes violent, sometimes loving, often
protective. Cuchullain refused her love and in her anger
she attacked him violently. Early in the fight Cuchullain
wounded the Morrígan, but gradually she got the better of
him. Many of his enemies moved in for the kill and when
he became weak from the onslaught, he strapped himself
to a pillar of stone and continued fighting until he died. A
black raven perched on his shoulder and an otter bit him
and drank his blood. Scholars argue about the bird; some
say it was the Morrígan, others that it was not.

The second story tells how Conor Mac Nessa, the
Ulster king, brought Cuchullain from Dundalk to
Eamhain Macha to protect him. Queen Maeve of
Connaght was approaching with her army to kill
Cuchullain. Clever Conor allowed his visitor to stay with
Niamh, his daughter-in-law. This woman of great beauty

was not beyond seducing a handsome warrior. Conor knew she would keep Cuchullain from joining in the fight when it began.

The grand-daughter of one of Cuchullain's early victims saw a chance for revenge. She placed a spell on herself, became exactly like Niamh and coaxed Cuchullain to fight. Being fond of a fracas, he needed little encouragement. He jumped into his chariot and slaughtered all around him. Still, age was beginning to tell, and he tired quickly. Lugaidh, the son of CúRoi, a man treacherously slain by Cuchullain years before, first killed Cuchullain's charioteer and then cast his spear, badly wounding Cuchullain.

Military nobility demanded that his enemies should allow the wounded warrior to drink. Cuchullain crawled to a lake, took his draught, and then called upon Lugaidh and his men to finish him off. Not wishing to die ignobly, however, he dragged himself up against a stone pillar and strapped himself to it with his sword belt. His enemies still feared him and kept their distance until a black raven perched on the great warrior's shoulder, pecked at it and drank his blood. This was a sure sign of death. They were relieved, because they would not really have relished ending a valiant life.

FOURTEEN

Oisín in Tír na nÓg

The grave of Queen Maeve of Connaght lies beneath a mound of stones on top of Knocknarea near Sligo. On the other side of the town stands gaunt, grim Ben Bulben, a table mountain associated with many legends. The best known of these concerns Oisín, son of Fionn Mac Cumhaill.

Between periods spent in the form of a doe, Sadbh, the deer goddess and daughter of the Munster king Bódearg, became mistress to Fionn. As a result of a curse placed on her by the wicked Dubhdraoí (Dark Druid), this woman could adopt human or animal forms. Fionn was hunting on the slopes of Ben Bulben one day and came across a young boy being suckled by a deer. It was his own son, and the deer was Sadbh. Fionn called the lad Oisín (Small Deer). When this handsome redhead approached manhood, he was already a great warrior and the chief bard of the Fianna. Many of his songs concerned his mother, who never again appeared in human form:

I sought the enchanted kingdom
In my dreams.
Finding it, I entered,
But only in my dreams.

Fionn was immensely proud of his son until he refused to be part of his father's scheme to capture Díarmuid and Gráinne after their elopement. Still they hunted together, for Fionn knew his son could track a deer or sense the presence of a wolf better than any of his warriors. Resting by the shores of Lough Léne in Killarney one day, father

and son saw a white cloud approaching swiftly across the
water. From its flimsy mist appeared a white stallion ridden
by a beautiful golden-haired young woman. It was Niamh
Cinn Óir (Niamh of the Golden Hair), daughter of the
sea-god Manannan Mac Lir. She wore a crown and a dress
of expensive green silk. The horse's shoes and harness were
pure silver, with bells that made ethereal music as the steed
galloped noiselessly towards the waiting warriors.

She told the men who she was, adding that her father
was king of Tír na nÓg. Fionn was dumbfounded. He had
often heard of this mystical Land of Eternal Youth and
longed to visit it, but the beautiful visitor issued her invitation to Oisín:

Come with me to my land of dreams,
Of emerald fields and silver streams;
Where songs in happiness are sung,
Sweet Land of Forever Young.
For years I've watched from distant parts
And loved you in my heart of hearts.

When he heard this, Fionn's emotions wavered between
jealousy at having to stay behind and sadness at Oisín's
departure. He knew that nobody could possibly refuse an
invitation to visit Tír na nÓg, especially when it came
from such a fair goddess. Oisín jumped upon the horse,
behind Niamh, and wound his arms around her waist. He
assured his father that he would return, but Fionn did not
believe him. The cloud reappeared and enveloped the
couple as they moved away. The sun became golden and
its rays almost blinded Fionn as he strained to watch his
son and Niamh disappear over the horizon.

Everything about that long ride was wonderful for
Oisín. He saw castles of silver, surrounded with orchards

full of golden apples. Some dwellings were large, some
tiny. Strange beasts, the like of which he had never
witnessed in Ireland, roamed the fields. Once he
attempted to question Niamh, but she warned him not to
speak again until she told him, or some great harm would
come to him. Eventually, the horse stopped and the pair
dismounted. Niamh kissed Oisín and welcomed him to
her enchanted land.

Here, things were even more wondrous and beautiful
than what Oisín had already beheld. Strange fruit and
crops abounded; people laughed and sang. There was
music everywhere, although no musicians were apparent.
The sky was not blue, but a delicate shade of pink. The
trees had leaves like velvet. Precious gems decorated the
walls of castles and cottages. Entering one, Niamh's palace,
Oisín saw rugs and furnishings with the most intricate
patterns, but one tapestry disturbed him. It showed a beautiful, mature woman's face on a white deer guarding a
hind that had long, human, red hair. After a while he
forgot about this and began to enjoy himself tremendously.

The pleasant environment and lively vivacity of Tír
na nÓg inspired Oisín to write more moving poems than
he had ever done before. They delighted Niamh Cinn Óir
and she made passionate love to her handsome Irish
warrior. They lived in great luxury and had nothing to do
all day but enjoy the splendour of their surroundings. No
two young lovers were ever so deliriously happy. Two
sons, Oscar and Fionn, and a daughter, Plúirín na mBan
(Small Flower of Women), were born to them, adding to
their joy.

One night Oisín dreamed of Ireland and of Fionn and
the Fianna. As if he was back, he wandered across the Hill
of Allen in County Kildare. He heard the baying of Bran

and Sceólan, Fionn's hounds, and the hunting horn of
former colleagues. Noticing their skill at fencing and other
athletic pursuits, he felt a longing for the more rugged but
adventurous life he had once enjoyed. He awoke to find
Niamh gazing fondly at him.

'What troubles you in your dreams?' she asked. 'For
many nights I have noticed your wrinkled brow and heard
your moaning sighs.'

Oisín wondered at this, for he could recall only one
dream. He told Niamh of it and, without thinking unduly,
suggested that he might go back to Ireland for a visit.

'I know nobody ever returned from Tír na nÓg,' he
said, 'but perhaps a beloved son of Fionn Mac Cumhaill
might be afforded the privilege?'

Because she still loved Oisín so much, Niamh could
not refuse, yet she feared for him. Nevertheless, the horse
upon which they had ridden into the enchanted land
appeared, fully saddled, and the couple kissed before
parting. Niamh whispered a warning not to dismount in
Ireland, but Oisín did not understand why. He sprang on
his steed and immediately a white cloud enveloped him. A
swift gallop across land and sea and suddenly there was the
western shore of Ireland with its sheer cliffs and lush green
fields above.

Oisín was delighted until he met a few people and
noticed that they were tiny compared to the men of the
Fianna. There were fewer forests and only once did he
hear the sounds of hunting horn or baying hounds. Instead
of running on foot after the fox like the hefty Fianna,
these small men rode horses and wore strange clothes.
They told him how to reach the Hill of Allen, but when
he got there, no great fortress was visible — just scrub,
briar and moss-covered ruins.

He called out loudly for Fionn, for Caoilte and for
Fionn's mistress Faolan, but there was no reply. Only
when he questioned a Kildare man did he realise that,
although his time in Tír na nÓg had seemed like only a
decade, three centuries had passed since he had ridden
away with Niamh Cinn Óir. In great sorrow, he rode
slowly towards the east, wishing to see as much of his
beloved country as possible before his return. Particularly
he wished to visit a beautiful spot near Dublin where the
Fianna used to rest, Gleann na Smól (Valley of the
Thrushes). When he reached it, he saw a group of men
attempting to move a large rock with crowbars. They
struggled and heaved and Oisín became sadder, for he
knew that a member of the Fianna could shift it with one
hand. To satisfy himself, he leaned down and, with one
hand, shoved the large boulder a hundred yards. If the
men marvelled at this feat of strength, they were dumbfounded at what happened next. The saddle-strap
broke and Oisín fell to the ground. In an instant, a virile,
handsome young warrior became a wrinkled,
horrible-looking old man.

Oisín knew then why Niamh had warned him not to
set foot on Ireland's soil. He whispered his story to the
men and they took him to Saint Patrick to repeat it.
The saint ordered his scribes to chronicle it for future
generations. One of these added a note that said he
believed the Fianna had never died but had hidden
themselves away in a magic cave, from which they would
emerge again in force when Ireland badly needed great
men. Perhaps they are overdue!

Glossary

Abhric	A farmer who befriended the four swans who were the Children of Lir.
Aengus Óg	The god of love who lived at Newgrange, County Meath.
Ail na Mireann	The Stone of Divisions. Said to have marked the junction of the five ancient provinces of Ireland and the centre of the country. It was known as the navel of Ireland.
Ailill	A number of characters bearing this name appear in Irish mythology. Ailill Mac Matha was King of Connaght.
Ainle	One of the sons of Uisneach.
Albha	Daughter of Ailill of Aran, foster-child of Bódearg.
Amhas	A hooligan or servant, hired to punish offenders.
Aobh	Daughter of Ailill, King of Aran and wife of Lir.
Aodh	One of the Children of Lir.
Aoife	Daughter of Ailill of Aran. The Children of Lir's stepmother.
Ardan	One of the Sons of Uisneach.

ball seirce	A beauty spot or love spot. A god could bestow it on a man, making him irresistible to women.
Balor of the Evil Eye	Formorian god of death, who lived on Tory Island off the Donegal coast.
barrabuadh	A bugle, horn or victory-horn.
Bobdall	A County Meath druidess, mentor to Fionn Mac Cumhaill.
Bódearg	The Red Bodb who succeeded Dagda as ruler of the gods. He lived at Killaloe, near Lough Derg, and was foster-father to the daughters of Ailill of Aran.
Bran	Fionn Mac Cumhaill's hound but also his nephew, born to Fionn's sister Tuireann, who had been turned into a bitch.
Brehon Laws	Derived from the Irish for a judge, *breitheamh*. The ancient Irish legal system was said to have been the oldest in the world.
Brúgh na Bóinne	Brugh (mansion or palace) of Boyne. Home of Aengus Óg, the god of love. Probably today's Newgrange.
caibosh	From the Irish *caipín* (cap) *bais* (death), therefore death cap. Many commentators say it is simply a colloquialism for 'kibosh' and it is indeed used in the same context.

Caol an Iarainn   (Iron Caol) Guardian of the Hound and the Gold Chain in Greece.

Caoilte Mac Rónan

        (*Caoilteamán*: a thin person). Cousin of Fionn Mac Cumhaill. Legend says he returned from the dead to acquaint Saint Patrick of the great deeds of Fionn and the Fianna.

Cathbad   A druid at the palace of Conor Mac Nessa, often alleged to be his father.

Conal Cearnach   Cuchullain's cousin and foster-brother. A celebrated Red Branch Knight who took the brain of a Leinster king (Mesgora) and made it into the brain ball that eventually killed Conor Mac Nessa.

Conán Maol   (Bald Conán) Conán Mac Mórna, member of the Fianna.

Conchobhar   (See Conor Mac Nessa.)

Conn   One of the Children of Lir.

Conor Mac Nessa   Usurper of the kingdom of Ulster during the Red Branch Cycle.

Cormac Mac Art   High King of Ireland, possibly during the third century A.D. The Fianna acted as his bodyguard.

Cuchullain   Culann's hound. Also known as The Hound of Ulster. Originally called Setanta, a youth who killed Culann's hound and volunteered to replace it by guarding Culann himself.

Cursing Stones   Stones said to be capable of placing a curse on seafarers if pointed towards their ship. The most famous of these were on Tory Island.

Dagda   Leader of the Tuatha Dé Danaan. The 'good god', leader, or father, of the gods.

Daire MacFachtna Original owner of the Brown Bull of Ulster.

Daman   Ferdia's father, who was a Firbolg leader.

Dana   A goddess after whom the Tuatha Dé Danaan are named.

Déirdre of the Sorrows
Daughter of an Ulster leader who refused to marry Conor Mac Nessa and eloped with Naoise, a son of Uisneach instead.

Deocha   Daughter of the King of Munster who sought the four swans, the Children of Lir.

Dian Cécht   The medicine god.

Díarmuid   Handsome member of the Fianna who eloped with Gráinne, Cormac Mac Art's daughter, because the aged Fionn wanted to marry her.

Don lionn iomhais   Liquid of inspiration. A magic potion that brought wisdom to those who drank it.

Donn Cuailng	The Brown Bull of Ulster, for possession of which the war of An Táin was fought.
Dubhdraoí	The Dark Druid, Fer Doirich.
Dun Cow	The Book of the Dun Cow is so called because its vellum came from a grey-brown cow.
Durtacht	Father of Eoghan, despised by Déirdre.
Eamhain Macha	Seat of the Kings of Ulster, near Armagh city.
Ebhla	Daughter of Cathbad and mother of Naoise.
Eithlinn	Daughter of Balor of the Evil Eye.
Eochaidh	Eochaidh Aireamh, a bachelor High King who fell in love with Étain.
Eoghan	Son of Durtacht.
Étain	Daughter of Ailill of Echraidhe in Ulster, she was changed into a butterfly by a druid at the request of Midir's first wife, Fuamnach.
Fear Ruadh	Red Man, a Scottish giant.
Fedlimid	The royal *seanchaí*.
Ferdia	Cuchullain's great friend. The pair fought at Ardee and Ferdia was slain.
Fergus McRoth	King of Ulster. He was tricked into giving the throne to Conor Mac Nessa.

Fiachra	One of the Children of Lir.
Fianna	Guardians of the High King of Ireland. They were recruited around 300 B.C., it is thought.
ficheall	A game like chess.
Finegas	Fionn Mac Cumhaill's tutor, who fished for the Salmon of Knowledge.
Finnabhair	Daughter of Ailill and Maeve.
Finnbheanach	A swineherd, turned into the White-Horned Bull of the royal herd in Connaght.

Fionn Mac Cumhaill

Leader of the Fianna. One of the most celebrated characters in Irish legend.

Fionnín	King of Munster, who tried to acquire the four swans, Children of Lir, for his daughter, Deocha.
Fionnuala	One of the Children of Lir.

Fios Fátha an Doimhin-Scéil

The Mystic Knowledge of the Deep Story. The tasks required to complete some heroic deed.

Firbolgs   The collective name for three groups of invaders. *Fir* means men and *bolg* means stomach or bulge, but some scholars explain that they were slaves in Thrace who were forced to carry clay in bags for reclaiming rocky mountain land.

Formorians	Evil gods, said to have congregated on Tory Island, County Donegal.
Fuamnach	Wife of Midir Mórálach.
gae bolga	'Belly spear'. Given to Cuchullain by Scáthac, it was kicked from the foot and opened into barbs when it entered an enemy's body.
geasa	A binding injunction.
Glasgamhan	Green calf.
Goibniu	The smith god.
Goll Mac Morna	Said to have killed Fionn Mac Cumhaill's father to gain leadership of the Fianna. He was succeeded in that appointment by Fionn.
Gráinne	Daughter of King Cormac Mac Art, who eloped with Díarmuid to avoid marrying Fionn Mac Cumhaill.
Hill of Uisneach	A hill near Ballymore, County Westmeath, site of a royal residence where great festivals were held. It was also a centre for paying levies.
Hy-Brasil	Originally the personal territory of the King of the World in the west of Ireland, the name was given to a blessed island that appeared in the Atlantic every seven years. The Irish once believed the Aran Islands to be remnants of Hy-Brasil.

Iollan the Fair   Son of Fergus McRoth.

Iuchar   One of the sons of Tuireann.

Iucharba   One of the sons of Tuireann.

Leaba Dhíarmada agus Gráinne
                     Diarmuid and Grainne's bed. Name
                     given to certain stone formations.

Leaba na Caillighe The woman's bed. Another name for
                     Diarmuid and Gráinne's bed.

Leabharcham   Governess at Eamhain Macha during
                     Conor Mac Nessa's reign as High King.

Lir   God of the sea, succeeded by his son,
                     Manannan. Lir's children were turned
                     into swans by his second wife.

Luacha   A County Meath druidess, mentor to
                     Fionn Mac Cumhaill.

Lug na Sionna   The Shannon Pot, source of the river.

Lugaidh   Lughaidh Mac ConRoi, son of CúRoi,
                     a man treacherously slain by Cuchullain
                     in the Ulster Cycle tale 'The Death of
                     CúRoi'.

Lugh   The sun god who killed his own grand-
                     father, Balor of the Evil Eye. He was
                     Cuchullain's father. He established the
                     pagan harvest festival of Lughnasa.

Lugh an Láimh Fada
                     Lugh of the Long Arm. A warrior god.

Maeve   Queen of Connaght, who went to war to gain possession of the Brown Bull of Ulster.

Mámuirthemne   A plain near Dundalk, County Louth.

Magh Tuireadh   The plain of towers, in the Mayo-Sligo area, where two great battles were fought.

Manannan Mac Lir

           Sea god and son of Lir who could change people's shapes. He drove his chariot across the waves.

meidir   A large wooden drinking cup with four handles, used for sharing drinks at banquets.

Midir Mórálach   Proud Midir. Tuatha Dé Danaan god and foster-father of Aengus Óg.

Mocaemhoch   Follower of Saint Patrick. He befriended the children of Lir and introduced them to Christianity.

Milesians   The last invaders of Ireland before the historical period.

Morrígan   The royal war goddess, said to have fomented the strife that brought about An Táin. Her aspect alters from legend to legend, however.

Naoise   The eldest of the Sons of Uisneach who eloped with Déirdre.

Niamh   Daughter of Ailill of Aran.

Niamh Cinn Óir Daughter of Manannan Mac Lir, who
                         brought Oisín to Tír na nÓg.

Nine Sacred Hazels
                         An enchanted copse near the source
                         of the river Shannon where the
                         Nuts of Knowledge grew. (See Well
                         of Connla.)

Oisín   Poet and Fianna warrior. Son of Fionn
                         Mac Cumhailll and Sadbh.

Oscar   Oisín's son. He was refused admission
                         to the Fianna, but he followed them
                         and came to their rescue one day. He
                         was then accepted and later became one
                         of their best fighters.

príomh-scéil   Main stories. Legends concerned with
                         great adventures, military actions,
                         voyages, romances and tragedies.

Red Branch Knights
                         Ridirí Craobh Ruadh. Guardians of Ulster.

Red Buinne the Ruthless
                         Son of Fergus McRoth.

Red-fisted Maine Son of the King of Norway.

Ros Dhá Roshoileach
                         Two Swallows Headland, thought to
                         have been in County Limerick.

Sadbh   The deer goddess and daughter of the
                         Munster king Bódearg. Fer Doirich, the
                         Dark Druid, turned her into a deer.

Salmon of Knowledge

A youth called Fintan ate the Nuts of
Knowledge and became a salmon. This
fish is associated with a story
concerning the source of the Shannon,
but mainly with the Boyne.

Scáthac   Scáthac Bhuachan (Scáthac of Victory),
who directed a military school on
Scáthac (sheltered) Island, probably
Skye, in Scotland.

Sceólan   Fionn Mac Cumhaill's second hound
and brother of Bran.

Sea of Moyle   The sea between Ireland and Scotland.

seanchaí   Storyteller.

Searbhán Lochlannach

The Bitter Marauder. A one-eyed ogre
who guarded a tree that bore magic
berries at Blackwood, County Mayo.

Setanta   Cuchullain's original name.

Sí Fionna   A *sí* was a 'fairy rath' or mound into
which the Tuatha Dé Danaan retreated.
Every god was given possession of one
by the Father of the Gods (Dagha). Lir's
was called Sí Fionna.

Sionnan   Daughter of Manannan Mac Lir (some
say of Lir's other son, Lodan). The river
Shannon is called after her because her
trespassing at the Well of Knowledge
brought about the river's formation.

Sons of Tuireann   This story resembles Jason's quest for the Golden Fleece.

Sons of Uisneach   Originally, the story was called *Oidhe Cloinne Uisneach* (The Tragic Tale of the Family of Uisneach).

Tailteann   Teltown, County Meath. Site of a great battle between the Tuatha Dé Danaan and the Milesians and location for a celebrated athletic event on the scale of the Greek Olympic Games.

Táin Bó Cuailgne   The Cattle-raid of Cooley. Irish mythology's greatest epic tale.

Teamhair   Tara, the capital of ancient Ireland and abode of her High Kings.

Three Sorrows of Storytelling
The Exile of the Sons of Uisneach, The Exile of the Sons of Tuireann and The Children of Lir.

Tír na nÓg   Land of Youth.

Tuatha Dé Danaan
Gods of pre-Christian Ireland.

Well of Connla   Well of Knowledge. Also Well of Segais. Situated at the Nine Sacred Hazels q.v. Given source of the rivers. Some claim that it was the source of the Shannon, others the Boyne.